W9-AWB-692

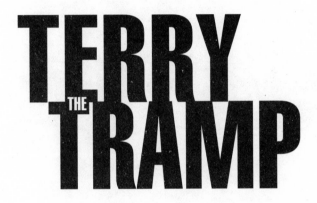

TERRY THE TRAMP

The Life and Dangerous Times of a One Percenter

K. RANDALL BALL

In Loving Memory of J.J.
August 24, 1948–December 27, 2010

We'll Never Forget You, J.J.

Ode to J.J.

Of all my many brothers
Who've ridden by my side
Whether living near or far
There is just one I can confide

His knees are always in the breeze
His face is in the wind
This brother has ridden further
Than the rest of us, my friend

Not just on the weekends
Not just to the store
Whether it's 100 degrees
Or a straight-up downpour

If his bike is down
It's no problem, you see
Cuz this brother is no dummy
He's got him two or three

So in recognition of brother J.J.
Who is always in the wind
He's put more miles on this motorcycle
Than he put on any girlfriend

Hey, that is no small feat, my brother
So it's with respect we say
We always give what we get
Yes, that's the Vago Way!

First published in 2011 by MBI Publishing Company LLC and Motorbooks, an imprint of MBI Publishing Company, 400 First Avenue North, Suite 300, Minneapolis, MN, 55401 USA

All photos from the Terry Orendorff collection unless otherwise noted.

The information in this book is true and complete to the best of our knowledge. All recommendations are made without any guarantee on the part of the author or Publisher, who also disclaim any liability incurred in connection with the use of this data or specific details.

We recognize, further, that some words, model names, and designations mentioned herein are the property of the trademark holder. We use them for identification purposes only. This is not an official publication.

MBI Publishing Company titles are also available at discounts in bulk quantity for industrial or sales-promotional use. For details write to Special Sales Manager at MBI Publishing Company, 400 First Avenue North, Suite 300, Minneapolis, MN, 55401 USA

ISBN-13: 978-0-7603-4005-9

Editor: Darwin Holmstrom
Design Manager: Kou Lor
Layout by: John Barnett, 4Eyes Design
Cover designed by: Rob Johnson, Toprotype, Inc.

On the front cover: *Photo copyright © 2011 Bill Tinney*

On the back cover: Terry and the Vagos visiting Silver in prison. *Photo copyright © 2011 Silver*

Printed in The United States of America

10 9 8 7 6 5 4 3 2 1

CONTENTS

PREFACE

Why Motorcycle Clubs?

I WAS A CHILD OF THE SIXTIES, born in 1948, one year after Terry the Tramp, the subject of this book. Like Terry I lived through the massive social changes that took place after World War II and throughout the sixties, and like Terry, I became immersed in the culture of motorcycle clubs. As I got into writing this book, it became apparent that the societal changes occurring when Terry and I were young were reflected within the changes that occurred in the motorcycling culture, and particularly in motorcycle clubs. Why did clubs change from straight-laced guys and couples in matching pressed uniforms into absolute wild men on bobbers, then choppers, wearing wild, unruly mountain-man attire?

I dug into our ugly history as far back as the 1930s, a time when you weren't shit unless you were born into the correct family, went to the right school or church, had the appropriate shade of skin pigmentation, and lived in an upscale neighborhood on the right side of the tracks. The Depression hit like a financial sledgehammer in the early thirties and society flipped upside-down. We were still reeling from the worst financial chaos in our country's history a decade later when we found ourselves being dragged into a world war. By the end of 1945, we had endured ten years of severe economic depression, followed by four years of violent global conflict.

When men returned from the war, they returned forever changed. Some were able to assimilate back into society, but for others, the societal norms and family ties that once shaped their every action no longer held the social leverage and power they had before the war. Many men found themselves unwilling to accept the rigid class structure society enforced in the pre-war years. Men from all social strata had fought side-by-side; in the battlefields of Europe and the Pacific, class structure had been replaced by military ranks. Pressure came from officers, regardless of what social class that man had been in prior to the war. When these men returned to the United States, they were no longer willing to accept the station of life into which they had happened to be born. When an American returned home after experiencing the horrors of war, no one was going to tell him what he could or could not do.

Many men found themselves unwilling to accept the rigid class structure that society had enforced in the pre-war years.

Motorcycling had been hugely popular in the early years of the internal-combustion engine. At that time automobiles were primarily expensive, one-off vehicles, hand-built by artisan coachbuilders. Motorcycles presented an inexpensive alternative to these pricey conveyances. That all changed when Henry Ford introduced the Model T, a mass-produced production-line vehicle that sold for less than many motorcycles. From the minute the Model T hit the market, motorcycle sales began to fall.

This slide in motorcycle sales picked up steam during the recession. At the peak of the motorcycling boom there were hundreds of motorcycle manufacturers in the United States; by the time the Great Depression had taken hold that number dwindled to three—Harley-Davidson, Indian, and Excelsior-Henderson. Within a couple years Excelsior-Henderson closed up shop, leaving just two.

But the war opened motorcycling to a broad audience as young men were drafted by the tens of thousands, and many thousands more volunteered to fight. Many of these young people learned how to ride motorcycles at training centers throughout the country. Young soldiers were taught to operate motorcycles for the Motor Transport Division, Signal Corps, Military Police, and numerous other branches. Army procurement officials hired former competitive riders, dealers, salesmen, and motorcycle mechanics to act as civilian instructors, introducing thousands of enlisted men and noncommissioned officers to motorcycling.

This influx of new riders proved a very good thing for the motorcycle industry. These new riders had cash to spend; after the war, Americans had discretionary income for the first time in two decades. Many Americans feared that the end of World War II and the subsequent drop in military spending might bring back the hard times of the Great Depression. Instead, pent-up consumer demand fueled exceptionally strong economic growth in the postwar period. The automobile industry successfully converted back to producing cars, and new industries such as aviation and electronics grew by leaps and bounds. A housing boom, stimulated in part by easily affordable mortgages for returning members of the military, added to the expansion. At the same time, the jump in postwar births—the baby boom that occurred after vets returned home and began breeding prolifically—increased the number of future consumers.

At the time the American Motorcyclist Association—the AMA—was ruled under the iron fist of one E.C. Smith, who served as the general secretary of the organization from 1928 until 1958. The AMA dictator wasn't terribly impressed with the behavior of many of these new riders, many of whom tried to recreate the excitement and thrills of their wartime adventures aboard their motorcycles. In the face of an increasingly unruly group of young riders, Smith stressed rules and regulations. In a lengthy speech to the AMA membership, he harped on expansion of the domestic motorcycle market in view of the fact that motorcycling in the United States. was centered on sporting and recreation, because the automobile had eclipsed the motorcycle's utility and transportation applications. Smith tried to sever ties to Canadian competitive riders because of their predilection for FICM rules, which allowed them to ride British bikes. He wanted to limit AMA activities north of the border to clubs that favored American machines for competition.

In 1942, Arthur Welch, the editor of *Motorcyclist*, was contracted to run a small ad for a foreign brand of motorcycle in the January 1943 edition. *Motorcyclist* was the only motorcycle magazine in the country, and was still controlled by the AMA at that time. Smith telephoned Arthur Welch from Columbus and reamed him a new one, stating that he was doing the American motorcycle industry a disservice by promoting information that might encourage the purchase of foreign machines. This heavy-handed approach did not sit well with Welch, and as the war was winding down in 1945, *The Motorcyclist* broke its bonds with the AMA and became an independent magazine. It proclaimed that it would be independent of industry control, and henceforth would be "Free, Fearless and Fair."

Smith started publishing his *AMA Report*, urging clubs that had disbanded during the war to reactivate and recruit new members. He immediately kicked off a new Competition Committee, which he chaired, and in 1946 stood ready with his staff at the Columbus offices of the AMA to develop an annual event schedule. In October 1946, he called a meeting of the Competition Committee. The members consisted of Harley-Davidson dealership owners only. No active competition riders were invited to the meeting.

The agenda called for a vote to publish a new competition rule book, which included enhanced enforcement of novice, amateur, and expert class categorizations. There would be no more lax AMA officials or referees.

Smith and his gang of H-D dealers had the audacity to pass and publicly announce a new Class C-mandated, lower-compression ratio of 6.5:1. The AMA piously described this change as a safety measure, but actually it was aimed at eliminating British machines from any Class C competition. The Brit bikes' overhead-valve 500 cc engines would not run well at compression ratios under 7.5:1. England almost single-handedly held the Nazis at bay for years, until the United States was attacked at Pearl Harbor, but the AMA, Harley-Davidson, and what remained of Indian by that time prevented them from racing or joining the AMA in America. Great bunch of guys.

When the AMA instituted anti-British racing rules, Welch tried to remain neutral and soft-pedal his differences with AMA policies, but hundreds of letters poured into his office disputing the new rule. The rules also drove a wedge between the AMA and Canadian competitors. Pouring fuel on the fire were Harley-Davidson clubs that restricted their competition activities to Milwaukee-made products only.

After the war the barriers against importing motorcycles began to fall, but there weren't many motorcycles worth importing being built anywhere in the lean post-war years. New bikes began to hit our shores in 1946, but they were generally pre-war designs.

The continuation of restrictive wartime rationing of materials delayed the resurgence of motorcycle manufacturers after the war. During the war folks couldn't stroll into any shop and buy sugar, butter, or meat. They couldn't fill up their gas tanks and drive wherever they wanted. Shortly after the first of May 1942, the U.S. Office of Price Administration (OPA) froze prices on most everyday goods. Gasoline, tires, sugar, meat, silk, shoes, and nylon were restricted. More than 8,000 rationing boards across the country were created. They even rationed farm equipment.

A certain amount of rationing continued even after the war because many of the materials needed for industry in the United States were being used to rebuild the war-torn European countries. In the grand hierarchy of priorities, motorcycle manufacturers worldwide were fairly low on the totem pole when it came to doling out steel, chrome, and other resources.

Something had to give—the bikes being produced by Harley-Davidson and Indian (especially Indian) didn't meet the needs of many riders as well as some of the foreign bikes, especially the hot-rod roadsters being built in England. The California-based British Motorcycle Dealers Association (BMDA) called for an emergency meeting in 1946 and voted unanimously to organize nationwide. Deciding that there was strength in numbers, they would present a united front against Smith, the AMA, and the Competition Committee.

In 1946, the same year that the British motorcycle dealers organized against the tyranny of Smith and the AMA, a new breed of outlaw motorcyclist began to make its presence known. These wild men and their stripped-down domestic V-twins started becoming a decidedly anti-social presence at AMA events. For the first time they were branded outlaws, and motorcycling started to generate a roughneck reputation.

Media reports blamed disillusioned ex-servicemen for the disreputable behavior. The rowdy behavior of this new breed of motorcyclist seemed especially startling when compared to the timid behavior of mainstream society at that time. *Time* magazine famously observed of those coming of age in the 1950s, "The most startling thing about the younger generation is its silence."

That wasn't the case for bikers. They started pushing the limits at AMA events such as the 1947 races in Daytona, Florida, where motorcyclists sped through the streets, rapping off loud pipes and generally raising hell. Groupies showed up in droves and erotic entertainment was unlimited.

Then on July 4, at the AMA's annual races and Gypsy tour at Hollister, California, an event occurred that would forever change the face of motorcycling. In 1947 a rowdy group of bikers decided to crash the party in the remote agricultural community. Things got a little out of hand, a few bikers were arrested for public intoxication and public urination, and the straights attending the AMA festivities grumbled a bit. That would have been the end of it, had the misadventures of the motorcyclists not landed on the pages of *Life* magazine. *Life* published a sensationalized account, going so far as to stage photos of a local dude posing aboard one of the bobbers parked on the street. The published images seem tame today, but in the repressed atmosphere of the 1950s the *Life* piece was positively shocking.

Men who had watched their brothers being blown to bits in the hedgerows of France and the islands of the Pacific were not shocked as easily as the general population. Rather than being appalled by the events at Hollister, many of these men wanted a piece of the action. Hollister may have frightened the straights, but it also sold a lot of motorcycles.

"There were no excuses, no laments, no protests," Bill Hayes wrote in his book *The Original Wild Ones*. "The country needed young soldiers. They went. War changes everyone. And everything. When young vets like Willie Forkner, Robert Burns, and George Manker (Booze Fighters) returned home, it was difficult to forget the horrors of what they had seen. It was hard to shake off the ingrained military regimentation. It was impossible to shed some of the cold-sweat guilt that comes with surviving while so many others did not. And there was an unnerving restlessness in trying to adapt to the calmness and serenity of 'normal' living after drowning in chaos. It was easy, however, to adopt an 'I don't fit in' kind of attitude. It was easy for returning vets to feel more comfortable with one another than with those from 'the outside.' "

In 1947 a rowdy group of bikers decided to crash the party ... Things got a little out of hand.

While motorcycling brothers were beginning to run wild in the streets, the AMA still sought to exert iron-fisted control over every aspect of the motorcycling world. Smith and company condemned the actions of the rowdy bikers and tried to ban anyone not connected with the AMA mafia from attending racing events. The organization also sought to control all media stories that, in any way shape or form, related to motorcycling. They outright threatened any publishers who even considered writing about non-American motorcycle brands. When R.W. "Pop" Cassell, born in England, tried to publish *Buzz-zz Motor Cycle News*, Smith told him that the AMA would not deviate from its long-standing policy of managing the news of the sport and industry. No derogatory editorializing or criticism of AMA or Competition Committee policies would be permitted, and all technical material was subject to prior review by the factory in question before being printed.

Shortly thereafter the AMA launched its own official publication, but it rapidly lost ground. Robert B. Petersen bought the foundering *Motorcyclist* magazine and added it to his stable that included *Motor Trend*, *Hot Rod* and *Kustom Kar*. Petersen's publishing empire was too big for even E.C. Smith to control; *Motorcyclist* magazine would publish stories on whatever brand of motorcycle it wanted regardless of country of origin, and if E.C. Smith or Harley-Davidson didn't like it, they could just kiss Robert B. Petersen's pearly-white ass. Once a mainstream business like Petersen Publishing got into the motorcycle magazine business, the floodgates opened. Suddenly American consumers were learning about motorcycle brands they hadn't even known existed just a few years earlier.

At the same time the AMA was losing control over the press, it was also losing control over the average American motorcyclist. Bikers returned from World War II as disillusioned with the AMA as they were confident in their mechanical abilities. Many of these young men formed clubs that the AMA would not approve of, to put it mildly. One year after the Hollister incident, the Hells Angels were born in San Bernardino. The HAs were just one of hundreds of such anti-authoritarian motorcycle clubs that formed, much to the chagrin of one E.C. Smith.

Still, most motorcyclists toed the AMA line. Apparently the bikers of 1947 were still intimidated by the Man. You can't blame people too much; those were intimidating times. We rolled directly from World War II into a Cold War. The iron curtain spread across Europe and we were suddenly embroiled in an international conflict over ideology. It was a perfect situation for megalomaniacs and tyrants who wanted to lord it over their fellow man. Over and over, these control freaks preyed on people's fear of that which was different—in this case Communism, but they also used the same tactics against bikers—and goaded the public into overreacting and causing their own worst nightmares. People wanted to be free no matter what, but the people instigating the mass hysteria of the era tricked them into forfeiting the very freedom they craved. The cops, bureaucrats, government agents, and control freaks spouted the rhetoric of freedom in every speech, but restricted freedom with their every action. Eventually their whole restrictive house of cards crashed around them, but in the process they destroyed many, many lives.

This world of tyrannically enforced conformism was not an ideal place in which motorcycling could thrive. The motorcycle industry fell on hard times. Indian shut down production in 1953, and Harley-Davidson faced hard times, in part because neither manufacturer would build the middleweight motorcycles the market demanded, as evidenced by the success of middleweight bikes from Triumph, BSA, and Royal Enfield. Harley

Bikers returned from World War II as disillusioned with the AMA as they were confident in their mechanical abilities.

went so far as to order all its dealers not to sell Cushman motorcycles, which would have afforded them a solid line of entry-level motorcycles to offset the small bikes that would soon start to trickle in from Japan.

With a population that feared them, a motorcycling hierarchy that hated them, and an industry that refused to build the kind of bikes they demanded, it's no wonder returning vets went outlaw, modified their bikes, and said to hell with the society they risked their lives for. The AMA pulled one underhanded act after another in an effort to control the market and the competitive arena, and many riders had had their fill. AMA membership slipped and Gypsy tours and clubs languished, while the outlaw spirit grew and began to take over.

Bob McMillen, a member of the Yellowjackets in 1946, remembered the AMA antics. "We weren't protesting," Bob said. "We were just having a good time and didn't like rules." Guys who wanted to compete tried to follow the rules, but the rebel notion was spreading like locusts over a field of produce.

The AMA's Smith and his Competition Committee tried their damnedest to maintain control of the sport. In 1950 they took it upon themselves to cheat Dick Klamfoth, the rider of the year, out of his official accolades, simply because he won a string of Midwest circuit races and the Daytona 200 on a Norton. Postcards and letters streamed into the AMA's Columbus offices in support of Klamfoth, but Smith and his gang of H-D dealerships chose to ignore the votes and announce that there would be no rider of the year declaration for 1950.

Smith claimed that there were insufficient votes to warrant the award presentation. Behind the curtain, he said that the award was only designated for riders of domestic machines. Downright hostility brewed between domestic and imported machine owners.

In spite of all this, motorcycling increased in popularity. U.S. sales numbers for 1950 were three times that of 1940, with Triumph the sales leader.

By 1958, the AMA Gypsy Tour was phased out because of the growing outlaw element. That year E.C. Smith finally retired and took home all his secret files, correspondence, and meeting minutes, along with financial records of his involvement with Milwaukee. Shortly thereafter the new AMA boss, Lin Kuchler, faced problems with the Internal Revenue Service. Seems when the AMA incorporated in 1928 they filed as a non-profit. But that didn't apply to the Class C concept kicked off in 1933. Income from the sanctioning body was never reported. Kuchler cut an annual payment deal with the IRS to prevent the AMA's demise.

As the 1950s gave way to the 1960s, motorcycling had earned a bad rap on two fronts. Outlaws were running amok, and the AMA itself had become something of a criminal organization, thanks to the shady bookkeeping of the E.C. Smith era. To make matters worse, the fratricidal warfare between Harley-Davidson and the foreign makes continued unabated.

> By 1958, the AMA Gypsy Tour was phased out because of the growing outlaw element.

Following Smith's departure the AMA began mending fences. Kuchler began a national public relations campaign and began to work with import manufacturers. In 1958, for the first time in history, riders on British machines claimed half of the national victories. This was the first time Milwaukee failed to win a majority. The AMA could no longer be considered a private club run for the benefit of Milwaukee.

As the 1940s gave way to the 1950s, the wild motorcycle club culture became more of a reaction against the constricting conformity society demanded during that era. The members of the outlaw clubs were uniquely positioned to take advantage of the hell that was about to break loose in the 1960s.

The 1960s was more of an idea than a time period. For starters, the decade didn't really begin in 1960. Really, it began after the assassination of President John F. Kennedy in November 1963. About that time everything started to change. The war in Vietnam began to ramp up. The civil rights movement picked up steam. Even the music changed. Jimmy Gilmore and the Fireballs' "Sugar Shack," and Little Peggy March's "I Will Follow Him," gave way to Bob Dylan, the Beatles, the Rolling Stones, Jimi Hendrix, Janis Joplin, and the Who. Sock hops and malt shops gave way to love-ins and hippy communes.

Not everyone joined the counterculture, and things didn't change overnight, but for the first time it wasn't just bikers who were fed up with the bullshit and sought out their own paths. Soon it seemed like every kid in every middle-class suburb in every major metropolitan area in the country was a rebel.

What they were rebelling against was anyone's guess. It's easy to understand the behavior of the returning vets in the crazed era that followed World War II, but most of the kids born during the baby boom couldn't blame deprivation or post-traumatic combat stress. Nor could they claim to rebel against the strict dictates of the AMA; most of them didn't even know about the mandated AMA structure and the nasty moves Harley-Davidson and Indian conjured up to keep Triumph and BSA off the shores of the USA. If you had asked a young person of the period why they were rebelling, chances are you wouldn't even get as satisfying an answer as Marlon Brando gave in the film, "The Wild One:" "What have you got?"

This is the world that spawned motorcycle clubs like the Vagos. This was the wild world in which Terry the Tramp grew to be a man. These tempting times led him to the world of outlaw bikers. ☠

INTRODUCTION

A Leader Was Born on the Wrong Side of the Tracks

THE HIGH DESERT WIND WHIPPED the fine sand along Sultana Road in Hesperia, California. Dust devils danced along the rural street lined with half-acre ranch style homes, forty miles south of Barstow, on Interstate 15 aimed at Vegas. The asphalt street was a dried-up river of mud, gouged by recent torrential downpours. One lane was destroyed, much like Terry the Tramp's rained-out life.

Terry, a forty-year member of the Vagos Motorcycle Club, was the club's boss and had been the international president for twenty-six years. As he sat in his stark home, the kitchen smelling of cigarette smoke and brewing coffee, he worried about paying the bills.

He was once the boss of the fastest-growing outlaw organization in Southern California. From dawn to dusk he handled club business, built chapters, stood up to some of the baddest one-percenters in the country, flew to wherever members needed him, and rallied the troops when the shit hit the fan. That was his life's mission until 2010.

Terry wasn't a big man, barely five-feet, nine-inches tall, narrow of frame with a potbelly that made him look like a renegade Buddha with scraggly, long gray hair, a bald top, and a serious paunch. He smoked one Marlboro after another while gulping strong cups of Folgers medium-roast coffee laced with hazelnut cream powder.

He was once the boss of the fastest-growing outlaw organization in Southern California.

The sixty-two-year-old faced jail time for the first time in his life. With thinning hair and a massive heart attack behind him, he still had fire in his dark green eyes and the one-percenter code etched into his heart.

At one time he ran with the Hollywood elite, married a multimillionaire, and saved her life a couple of times. But as he faced a prison sentence because he couldn't afford to pay a federal fine, he looked at an empty bank account and worried about his son's well-being. He raised the boy from the time that the boy's mother decided she could no longer stand bikers and left.

Terry's home, clean as a whistle, was decorated in a western motif, including paintings of the West, American Indian artifacts, and prints of John Wayne hanging on the white walls. His well-organized garage held remnants of a shop he owned, operated, and closed, as well as used tools he occasionally sold to pay the mortgage and keep the lights on.

After too many raids on his home, he finally hid all club-related paraphernalia in a far-away storage locker for fear of losing it. The '59 Panhead he owned for thirty years was stashed in the storage locker alongside his club photos and memorabilia.

At one time his life was harried and constantly on edge, but not in April of 2010. His club had changed and he unknowingly relinquished his position as the international president while he waited outside a downtown Los Angeles federal courthouse for final sentencing after a decade-old indictment came to fruition.

"A federal indictment has no statute of limitations," Terry said. "They can hang on to an indictment forever."

The paper accusation was filed in 2001. His home was raided during a statewide sweep in 2006, and after years of searching his tax records, the district attorney finally discovered enough evidence of tax evasion to drag Terry in front of a federal judge.

For forty years he sold motorcycles to bail out brothers, mustered legal teams, prevented wars with other one-percenter clubs, and held chapters together during hard times. As Terry faced this stoic judge in a cold, granite federal courthouse adorned with fluted pilasters in downtown Los Angeles, the magistrate reviewed Terry's extensive criminal file and looked down at the old outlaw with the long gray Fu Manchu mustache.

"I believe I'm looking at a professional crook," the judge said.

"I made a deal for no jail time," Terry said. But in federal court, a judge is not bound by the deals made between the district attorney and the defendant in private chambers. After forty years on the toughest streets in the nation, Terry stood with just one faithful brother, Billy, at his side. His club had turned against him and his support group was gone, but what a ride it had been.

"This is my courtroom, and he's going to prison," the judge snapped after reviewing the case. He smacked his gavel against the mahogany sound block to punctuate his ruling.

What makes a man a leader? What drives him to step up during turbulent times and take the reins of a one-percenter motorcycle club? What gives him the strength to deal with potentially violent situations made even more dangerous by mind-altering drugs used by the men involved? What level of confidence calms a man's heart while surrounded by men looking for any excuse to kill?

Ultimately, Terry became the international boss of one of the most notorious motorcycle clubs of them all, a club that rocked southern California, spread to several states, and even reached Japan and Mexico. ☠

> His club had turned against him, his support group was gone, but what a ride it had been.

The Unlikely Leader

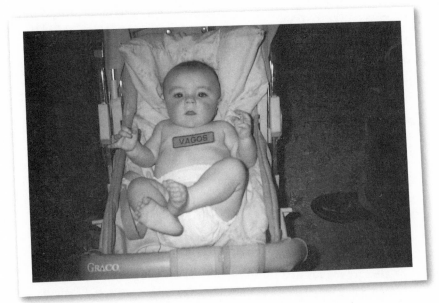

TERRY "THE TRAMP" ORENDORFF was born in 1947—smack in the middle of the baby boom generation—in El Monte, California. El Monte is just south of downtown Los Angeles off the notorious I-10 freeway out of Santa Monica, the highway destined to replace U.S. Route 66 as America's main coast-to-coast route of choice. Terry's German-born father, Edwin Eugene, was no more than a memory, a drunk who abandoned his two children to seek an actor's fame in Hollywood. Terry met him only once. Terry was fourteen at the time, with slick coal-black hair combed into a pompadour, wearing Levi's and a dirty white T-shirt, facing charges for street gang activity in a cold, slate-and-concrete Los Angeles courtroom. For a brief moment he faced his seven-foot two-inch father, who was being arraigned for failure to provide child support.

"You can call me Dad," the big man said and attempted a brief smile.

Spider, a member of the Victorville chapter, once a member of the Berdoo Charter, at a party with his new son, sixteen years ago. Showing Vago pride even as a youngster.

Terry's German-born father, Edwin Eugene, was no more than a memory, a drunk who abandoned his two children to seek an actor's fame in Hollywood.

"I'll call you anything but Dad," Terry spat.

He never saw his father again, and his mother never received a penny of child support. "I wanted to shoot him," Terry recalled.

As an infant, Terry met a man who would be a positive but notorious influence throughout most of his life. Harold Tuttle was the father of one of Terry's sisters, Mary Jane. Harold never married Terry's mother, Doris.

Harold was a bank robber who was in and out of prison. Harold's father ran with Pretty Boy Floyd. Harold spent more time locked up than walking the streets, but when he was out, he came around to see Doris, sometimes on a Harley-Davidson Knucklehead.

"He gave me my first ride on a Harley," Terry said.

One day when Terry was between five and six years old, a man came to their home and beat his mother. Shortly thereafter, Harold rolled up on his Harley.

When he saw the black and blue bruises on Doris, he asked Terry, "Kid, could you recognize the guy who did this?"

Terry nodded and Harold swept him up onto the large, fat bob gas tank for a rumbling ride to the Bell Ship Bar on Valley Boulevard in El Monte. Harold strolled into the dank saloon carrying young Terry and set him on top of the narrow bar.

"Just walk down the bar and point at the guy," Harold said.

Terry did as he was told. He walked tentatively along the slick bar-top surface, the smell of hard liquor and stale beer filling his nostrils for the first time. When he found the man draped around his frosty cocktail tumbler, he turned to Harold in the smoke-filled bar and pointed. While he stood in the darkened saloon, he watched the stocky five-foot, ten-inch Harold, his jet-black hair matching his bushy mustache, grit his teeth and approach the man. Harold yanked him off his barstool and beat him half to death on the grungy barroom floor. Harold stood up panting, stepped to the bar victorious, swept Terry into his arms and departed.

When Terry was eight years old, Doris married Everett, a thin, dour man who worked for the city of Los Angeles in a hydroelectric plant. Everett moved the growing family of five brothers and three sisters into a small house on Arden in El Monte, across from the Ball Jar manufacturing facility.

"Mom brought six kids," Terry said, "and Everett had four originally, but two sisters returned to New York."

Everett, a skinny, tall man, turned the garage, which was built against the alley, into a bunkhouse with a crude bathroom and laundry facility. The kids weren't allowed in the main house. They ate at a makeshift picnic table on the concrete floor in the garage and were forced to develop a strong sense of family survival, providing support for one another.

"The old hermit threw the light switch every night at six. It was lights out," Terry said. They weren't allowed in the house except once a week to watch an episode of the TV series, *Rawhide*.

"The old man bolted a padlock clasp on the refrigerator," Terry said, "so we had to earn money and buy our own snacks. He locked the bread supply in a tool box."

Only two of the boys, Steve and Terry, were blood relatives. Eddie (who also became a Vago) came to California from Oklahoma with his abusive folks.

"He started to come over to our place and ultimately moved in," Terry said. Carol, Sandy, and Mary Jane were also Doris's children. Frank was Everett's son, a twin, but his mother murdered his brother when they were infants in New York. She strapped the twins to a tree and beat one to death with a broom handle. Someone stopped her before she had the chance to inflict permanent physical damage to Frank, but the mental destruction had already taken place. The sordid group all lived together in the garage overlooking a dirt alley populated by passed-out drug addicts that ended in a vacant lot used by transient truck drivers.

She strapped the twins to a tree and beat one to death with a broom handle.

"My mom looked like Doris Day—she was a blonde—and she always tried to help us kids," Terry said. "She worked cleaning houses and bought us Goodwill clothes."

The diminutive, five-foot-tall Doris made quilted potholders that the kids sold door-to-door. Terry mowed lawns, cleaned horse stables, and raised and sold rats.

It was a strange time of pent-up desires, disillusionment, and unrealized American dreams. The World War was over. There were no more battles to win, but the warrior's desire smoldered in the souls of many men. Violence still filled the air. Baby boomers rejected or redefined traditional family values. Times were changing. Society experienced a new level of privilege and affluence and didn't know how to respond. This was the wealthiest and healthiest generation. Parents had been lost between Depression-era demands and war-year restrictions while they grew up, whereas the kids rocked out.

"Sirens wailed all night long," Terry said of his youth. Life in the garage was difficult, but Terry and his siblings rapidly developed a strong sense of comradeship, along with caring natures and nurturing spirits.

He ran a paper route with his sister near the Santa Fe Inn, where he was busted for stealing coins from the fountain.

"I took off my shoes, rolled up my Levi's, and waded into the long, lukewarm pool," Terry said. The dinner house where Terry was busted was built at the cow-town end of the famous Santa Fe Trail. The fountain, which featured a wooden water wheel and the concrete pool, ran the length of the building with a bridge arching over it. "That's where folks tossed their coins." On weekends, American Indians set up kiosks around the fountain, selling turquoise jewelry, Indian blankets, and terracotta pottery, attracting numerous patrons, and an abundance of coin-tossers made fountain deposits.

Terry wandered into the 18-inch-deep pool and gathered coins. It was his morning drill with his sister, just after their paper route. They hit a downtown coffee shop for cocoa and cookies after they scored a wet handful of change from the shallow pool.

"Nothing to it," Terry said, describing the routine. Except that on one morning as the sun crested the San Gabriel Mountains and

Terry pocketed another handful of slippery coins he turned to face a mountain of man in a freshly pressed, dark pinstriped suit. "He scared the shit outta me."

"What am going to do about this?" the big, middle-aged man asked while looking down at Terry, who stood knee-deep in the concrete pool surrounded by glistening coins. "You're stealing," he said, and his raised salt-and-pepper eyebrow indicated his disdain.

"I didn't think I was stealing," Terry said. "Folks tossed the coins in here for the taking, right?"

Terry could tell immediately from the big man's wrinkled brow that it wasn't the appropriate response. "That's not the case."

The big owner shuffled his polished wing-tip shoes on the pavement and slipped his left hand inside his coat pocket, as if he was reaching for a gun.

"I thought for sure he was going to call the cops," Terry said. His heart rate sped, then waned. He was just a little guy facing an uncertain judgment. He would never forget that morning and the level of dread he felt.

The man sensed Terry's remorse for his devious deed. "If I ever catch you stealing again," he said, "there will be hell to pay."

"You won't ever see us around here again," Terry said, clambering out of the fountain and jumping on his bike. His sister climbed onto the handlebars. "We hauled ass out of there. I never stole another dime."

Terry raised pigeons in the laundry shed and ducks in the backyard. Terry and his brothers and sisters basically lived unsupervised in the garage. As a result they saw things no child should ever have to see. For example, while playing war and building a fort in a vacant lot one day, Terry stumbled across his first dead body, a truck driver who had overdosed.

Finally Mrs. Cook, a local woman living at the end of the dirt alley, took Terry under her wing and made sure his brothers and sisters received birthday gifts.

"She was a sweetheart and took us to see the Roller Derby at the Olympic Stadium in downtown Los Angeles," Terry recalled. The kids were excited to see the famous T-Birds face off against the

While playing war and building a fort in a vacant lot one day, Terry stumbled across his first dead body, a truck driver who had overdosed.

wild Racing Blonde Bombers. They were teams of buffed and bodacious broads in skimpy outfits flying around the arena on steel skates, slipping, sliding, and wrestling each other against the stiff, slick, cambered hardwood velodrome track.

When he was nine, Terry felt another sting of violence in the notorious alley behind his house when he witnessed a gang beating.

"They used narrow belts to whip this guy," Terry said. He watched the group of hoods in white Penney's T-shirts, Levi's, and hard leather shoes surround their prey and knock him to the gravel and dirt of the alley. They unbuckled their belts, yanked them free of the denim loops, and whipped the young loner unmercifully.

Next door, Roy's dad Chuck beat his mom into abject submission. Chuck, a big, washed-out prize fighter, showed no mercy when he whipped his kids, Roy and Jim. It took six cops to wrestle him into a black and white after he beat his wife with his calloused fists. He was an angry drunk.

"It was three days before her eyes reopened," Terry said.

It was a time of raging emotions. Men felt like rudderless sailing vessels in a growing gale. They lacked a mission or a battle to win. The world lay at their feet, but presented no soldier's challenge. Times changed but they couldn't see the gleaming forest for the trees of past repressions.

At thirteen, Terry was beat up by two bullies in the alley and something changed forever in his psyche. His stepbrother Eddie, four years older, who became "Parts" in the Vagos, retaliated, but the way Terry viewed the world would never be the same.

As a matter of survival, he rapidly learned the body language of violence. One of Terry's stepbrothers, Frank, who was also four years older, couldn't take the ever-threatening Los Angeles streets. He ran away, changed his name, and never returned.

In Terry's world, violence was a force from which there was no permanent escape—only respite. Terry's drunkard stepdad pushed his mom around, and the relationship began to crumble.

"He ran the same drill every day," Terry said. "He came home from work, cleaned up, watched TV, and didn't say a word to any of us. Then he drank throughout every weekend."

Terry was developing an understanding of violence, how it worked, and how it didn't work.

It started at a local bar every Friday night. As the weekend rolled on, the trips to saloons increased along with the heated arguments. The relationship between Doris and Everett became more abusive until one hot afternoon when Terry was fourteen, he witnessed Everett shoving his mom around and stepped in.

"He tried to beat me with a baseball bat," Terry said. Violence had become a way of life for Terry, a gauge of a man's heart, his meaning, or his treachery.

At sixteen Terry was attacked in an alley while heading home from school and was beaten with tire irons. Again, Parts took care of the investigation and payback. Terry was developing an understanding of violence, how it worked, and how it didn't work. He quickly learned to judge how a confrontation was going down. ☠

Panheads and Punks

TERRY ORENDORFF DISCOVERED HIS FIRST MOTORCYCLE, an abandoned early 1950s Panhead Harley-Davidson, in Mrs. Smith's backyard down the dirt alley behind Arden Street in the San Gabriel Valley. The valley was the home of the first freeway in the nation, called the cycleway, in 1897, which became the Pasadena Freeway connecting Pasadena to downtown Los Angeles. He was just twelve years old and fascinated by the old Big Twin, a 74-cubic-inch monster.

With a wooden cart that he used to collect metal scrap, he hauled the big Harley home piece by piece. Harold Tuttle encouraged him to buy a two-dollar Harley-Davidson manual and he began to collect tools like they were gold coins. Terry stashed the Harley parts in the washer shed off the side of their dorm garage.

"My stepdad bitched about it when he got drunk on the weekends," Terry said.

An older, balding gentleman two doors away noticed Terry's struggling efforts with the motorcycle and loaned him tools.

At sixteen, Terry working in R-Town near San Luis Obispo, a makeshift town built specifically for television commercial production. The star for this series of commercials was Dale Robertson.

"Bring them back every night," Mr. Smith told the teen, "if you plan to use them tomorrow." Mr. Smith owned MG sportscars and constantly tinkered with them. He worked for Coca-Cola and brought home cases of the soft drinks for Terry's brothers and sisters. Terry dug into each motorcycle part with a wire brush and a can of gasoline.

Terry found a sense of accomplishment as he read the manual and tinkered with the big machine. He also discovered the nature of a biker's support group in the men who helped him learn to use tools, understand the inner workings of the beast, and oversee his growing knowledge about the big overhead-valve motorcycle.

But there was another side of Terry's life, the bully side. It was 1960 and the streets of Los Angeles ran rampant with violence. Kids picked on each other for being too tall, too short, too fat, too poor, too slow, too dumb, or too smart; it didn't matter. There were cliques of bully brothers, Hispanic gangs, punks, hoods, and thugs. A kid fought, got his ass kicked, or ducked confrontations constantly.

Terry's dad beat him at night, while the retired Marine who was his teacher at Charles E. Gidley Junior High School in El Monte barked disciplinary orders and smacked kids with his heavy gold Marine ring during school hours. Terry walked a mile to school every morning, only to be rat-packed by the Corbin brothers. Every day followed the same drill. If he caught the younger Corbin by himself, Terry kicked ass. If the two brothers caught up with Terry on his way home, he got his ass kicked. The Corbins also had a hang-around named Pat.

"He wasn't much of a fighter," Terry said, "but he had a big mouth, and it ran constantly."

One day Pat caught Terry alone in a classroom and mouthed off about Terry's mom. The fight was on, and Terry grabbed a pointed paperweight and stabbed Pat in the neck. Terry was immediately kicked out of school. He was shipped to a bad-boy, prison-like school called Columbia, one block from the El Monte cop shop. Within a week he was attacked in the Los Angeles River bed and beaten by three Columbia students on his way to school. Terry spotted them later in the day at recess and vowed to take revenge. A couple of hot

One day, Pat caught Terry alone in a classroom and mouthed off about Terry's mom. The fight was on, and Terry grabbed a pointed paperweight and stabbed Pat in the neck.

Los Angeles days later, on the smoldering asphalt grounds, he checked out a baseball bat and got even.

The next day, he mouthed off to Miss Isnick, who smacked him in the head with a book.

"Generally, if we were in trouble," Terry said, "we were ordered to stand alone in the empty halls, but not this time."

Miss Isnick hauled Terry to the principal's office. The short, grizzled, overweight principal told Terry to sit in his somber office. He retrieved a polished oak paddle from his closet and set it abruptly on his desk with a deafening smack.

"You know what this means, son," the balding principal said. "You just think about that, and I'll be right back."

The principal stepped away from his office momentarily, leaving the hardwood paddle on his vast oak desk. When he returned, Terry controlled the weapon and took a swing at the principal. He was sent back to Gidley Junior High.

Every night he found solace tinkering with the Panhead, scouring his two-buck manual, and learning about tools from Mr. Smith. At one point his sister showed up with a can of paint and two brushes. Together they painted the entire motorcycle pink. Terry quickly learned, through street communication, finger-pointing, and laughter, that pink wasn't a proper chopper color. Jerry and Eddie from the local Richfield station hooked him up with a rattle can of black spray paint and Terry transformed his first Harley from a ratty chick motorcycle to a badass bob job.

Harold Tuttle, his little sister's dad, helped him get it running. He showed him how to adjust the solid lifters, the carburetor, the points, and the spark plug gaps.

"The first time it fired, it roared and spit black smoke," Terry said. "I'll never forget that moment."

The air was filled with the smell of fire, fuel, and oil, but it also smelled of power, mobility, and freedom. A chill ran up Terry's spine as he rolled the big twin into the grassy dirt alley and practiced with the mousetrap-engaged clutch and foot shifter.

"I ran into a wooden fence at the end of the block," Terry said. The mechanical brakes were lousy. The old brake shoes no longer fit the scored contour of the mechanical brake drums. He learned how to adjust the brakes and attempted another run through the alley. As he dialed in the big Harley and built riding confidence he was able to roam farther from his digs, every night after school he pulled the big motorcycle out of the shed and blasted around town, through the back streets and alleys.

He was pulled over frequently by local cops.

> It was tough to get around a small town, especially when all the cops knew you, knew you were under-age, and that you had no license.

"It was tough to rumble around a small town, especially when all the cops knew you, knew you were under-age, and that you had no license. Besides, the motorcycle wasn't registered and had no plate or tags." Finally, the vintage Harley was impounded.

A Gidley teacher threw Terry out of her class for being a poor reader. Standing in the lonely hall, he refused to sit still. He pulled the fire alarm and was kicked out of school again. But he was invited back to graduate so he could move onto the rigors of high school education.

Then life took a fortuitous turn. After graduation, Terry's folks hauled the entire Orendorff, and Tuttle clan a couple blocks away from the low-life Arden Street area to Maxton Lane, on the edge of the highbrow side of town. There he met a girl who would impact his life forever.

The alley behind Maxton was unpaved dirt, like Arden, but occasionally horses trotted through the weeds. One summer day while listening to Roy Orbison crooning, "Only the Lonely" on a transistor radio in the backyard, he heard a girl call for help. She had tried to ride her horse through the alley and was accosted by a couple of punks with nothing better to do than harass the homely girl riding a high-strung mare.

Terry witnessed two teenagers throwing stones at the frightened Morgan. The mare snorted, reared, and dumped her rider in the gravel- and brush-strewn alley. Terry jumped the fence and chased the kids off. He helped the tall youngster to her feet and dusted her off. Her eyes were deep-set and her skinny form revealed an ugly, tomboy appearance. He helped her calm the stout animal, and they both climbed aboard for the short ride to her folks' home just a couple blocks away. Her name was Pam and like Terry, she loved animals. Melody, the skittish horse, bolted for the barn once it sensed its proximity to home base. Behind the stucco and western brick home, Melody skidded to a halt, dumping both kids in the dirt.

Terry stood, helped Pam to her feet once more, dusted himself off, and gazed around the half-acre lot surrounding the two-story western home. The yard contained a myriad of brick construction, antique cars, and fifty Indian motorcycles in various states of repair. Terry felt like he'd died and gone to heaven.

Pam's dad, Harry Woolman, worked for various movie and television studios as an actor, stuntman, and special effects coordinator. When he wasn't building sets, his trade was brickwork, which was evident around his home in the ornate planters, the driveway, and fireplace.

"I saw the most incredible things," Terry said. "There was a movie space ship in this guy's back yard. It was used in a movie called *Rock Ship*." A giant fuzzy tarantula collected dust in the corner of the yard, along with several Rock People mannequins. Terry didn't know which way to turn.

"Wanna earn some pocket money?" Harry asked Terry. "I'll pay you five bucks an hour to load bricks."

Harry was born and raised in Elkton, Maryland, an unassuming marrying

The yard contained a myriad of brick construction, antique cars, and fifty India motorcy s in various tes of repai t like Terry he'd d and gone eaven.

town where fifteen private chapels made Elkton the elopement capital of the East Coast. As a kid in the 1930s, Harry was the town guide, meeting young couples on the edge of town on his Indian motorcycle and escorting them to the chapel of their choice. During his tours he performed stunts on his flathead to the delight of customers from all over the East. One day he impressed a Hollywood producer with his wheel stands and balancing while riding and standing on his seat. He was invited to begin a career as a stuntman on the West Coast.

Harry worked on some of the last silent films. He developed a reputation as a stuntman and special effects innovator, doubling for such notables as Clark Gable, Charles Laughton, William Bendix, and John Carradine. He also appeared in occasional roles, such as a motorcycle police officer in an Abbott and Costello comedy. During the course of his film career, Harry survived more than 3,000 head-on collisions and was featured numerous times on the television program, *You Asked for It*, doing everything from jumping a house with a car to being blown up in a paper coffin by twenty sticks of dynamite. He jumped his own house with a 1956 Ford while one of his daughters tried to take a nap in the back seat.

Having gained practice in handling cars while running moonshine in rural Cecil County, Maryland, Woolman headlined as a thrill rider on the racetrack circuit with Ed "Lucky" Teter and his Champion Hell Drivers. A complex and changing cultural and political landscape defined the 1960s. Harry was ensconced in the Hollywood studio industry during this crazed era.

Harry's wife, Alma, a demure five-foot six-inch woman with sparkling eyes and a constant smile coupled with an upbeat personality, could have doubled for actress Lupy Valdez. Her parents were Greek immigrants who lived on the streets of Whittier, California, through the prohibition era of the 1920s. With an entrepreneurial spirit serving as a guiding light, Louis and Pauline Papas fulfilled their own vision of the American Dream. They owned a pool hall and a barber shop on Whittier Boulevard. A false wall in the barber led to a gambling den. They also owned a dance school and a cleaners. They invested in seaside apartment houses in Hermosa

Beach. Louie still enjoyed walks in the park and a game of nine-ball well into his nineties.

From the moment Terry met Pam and her folks, Harry and Alma, he found a surrogate family, a positive, prankster father figure, a vocation within the Hollywood studios, several trades, and an introduction to the Hollywood biker world.

Terry watched Pam grow from the gangly, homely girl who had been, thrown from her horse into a very different creature. Age and puberty transformed the girl, who was two years younger than Terry, from a twelve-year-old, skinny, angular tomboy into a knockout fourteen-year-old Hollywood actress.

"At thirteen, she started to change," Terry said, "By the time she turned fourteen, she was no longer an ugly duckling."

Pam was a passionate girl, a child of the sixties, unleashed by the urge to roam free. Though the family wasn't wealthy, Pam never went without. The day she received her driver's license, her folks hauled her and Terry to the nearest Los Angeles Ford dealership and bought Pam a brand-new, shiny, fire engine-red 1965 Mustang, with an all-black Naugahyde interior and bucket seats.

Seven months later, her dad destroyed the new Mustang while filming a commercial for Kool cigarettes. Terry helped Harry set up a series of special-effect jump ramps at a regional speedway. Harry tested Pam's Mustang around the track, while Donna, Pam's sister, drove another Mustang as the pace car.

"Harry instructed the tech to remove the air-conditioning from under the hood of Pam's car, but didn't confirm the operation. Harry later drove the flashy red Mustang around the track several times and attempted a jump off the ramp. The Mustang took a nosedive and was totaled.

"That was one of the rare times when I saw Harry blow up," Terry said. "He fumed and forced the techs to remove the air-conditioning from the backup Mustang."

Harry made five passes and five successful jumps in the backup car without a hitch. They towed Pam's Mustang back to town and rebuilt it completely, but it was never the same, so her dad bought her a new VW. ☠

The Panhead and the
Biker Movie

IN 1960 SMOKEY ROBINSON AND THE MIRACLES hit the Motown airways with their first hit, "Shop Around," Elvis was discharged from the army, and the rock and roll era hit full swing. That same year Terry was busted for stealing gas and busting curfew.

"I swear I didn't do it," Terry said. He was fifteen and hanging with some buddies, one of whom had borrowed his father's car, which they ran out of gas.

While Terry stood watch two of his buddies tried to siphon gas from a parked car when a black and white turned the corner.

"I'll run this way to draw them off," Terry volunteered, and he took off. The cops gave chase and apprehended him. Later that night, the two friends were caught stealing gas. They were cut loose while Terry was hauled to juvenile hall and booked on a curfew violation.

His mom, Doris, reached her wits' end. Terry faced a formidable choice: go to juvenile hall or into foster care. Terry was assigned to the El Monte High School continuation school on Saturdays only.

On another studio job in the 1960s as a kid, Terry was learning grip duties during inset shots for a western. Note the pack of Marlboros in his Levi's pocket. He started early. He gave up a lucrative, fascinating studio career for the club.

Terry faced a formidable choice: go to juvenile hall or into foster care. Harry recognized Terry's wandering, renegade ways and put him to work full time. Terry moved away from his family on Maxton and the courts assigned guardianship to Harry and Alma Woolman. He became a foster child instead of being incarcerated in the juvenile hall detention center, which would have set him on a devious track to personal doom.

Terry loved his mom, Doris, but he had to escape from his bastard, abusive, drunken stepfather, Everett. Ultimately the couple broke up, but Terry's dedicated mother continued to look after Everett for twenty years until he died of cancer.

Living with Harry and Alma, Terry found himself in an entirely different, jubilant, creative atmosphere, one that encouraged learning, building, testing, social interaction, and constant creative exploits. A whole new world opened for Terry as he crawled into Harry's Ford grip pickup and rolled into Jack Miles's studio to work on a movie called *Push Button Honeymoon*. He learned brickwork, mechanics, construction, electrical work, respect for tools, and about being a prankster from Harry. It was nothing for Harry to pull a dynamite-based trick.

In 1965, during the Los Angeles riots, a car skidded to a stop in the street in front of Harry's house, where Terry worked on a 1960 two-door Dodge from a movie set. An angry young black man shot Terry from the window of his rumbling coupe. The bullet hit Terry in the hip and knocked him from the curb where he was crouched while trying to install new brake shoes. Terry flew back twenty feet to the stucco garage.

"Hubert, another local kid, was helping me out," Terry said, "but he didn't drive too well. We scrambled into an old car and he rear-ended another vehicle on Soto street before we reached the Santa Anita Hospital."

While Terry lay on a cold, stainless steel gurney in the emergency room, doctors told him the projectile was too close to his spine for surgical removal. He would be forced to wait until it dislodged itself before they could operate. He was given a stiff pain

An angry young black man shot Terry from the window of his rumbling coupe.

killer and released. A couple days later, he pulled into a Bells Olympic gas station to refuel. As he stood behind his Chevy, with the hose and spigot stuffed into his tank hosepipe, he twisted to look at the gas pump and the lead projectile shifted. He immediately slipped to the pavement, paralyzed from the hips down.

"I never experienced such a cold, helpless feeling," Terry said. Someone called an ambulance, which delivered him to Los Angeles General Hospital. He lay in the hospital as surgeons reviewed his X-rays, breathing in the smell of the surgical cleansing chemicals that filled the cold emergency room air, thinking he would never walk again. The doctors' dour body language betrayed their hopelessness as they pointed at the glowing film strips on the light table and shook their heads dismally.

Terry was petrified. He could not move. His legs had turned cold and lifeless. Then a new, tall surgeon arrived, pulled the wavy blue curtain aside, and stepped into his crowded area. He snatched one of the X-rays off the light box and studied it against the bright overhead lights.

"What are you waiting for?" the doctor asked. "Christmas?" Without hesitation he called for Terry to be rolled into surgery, demanding, "Get the sheriff in here." (By law, a cop had to be present when a bullet was removed.)

Nurses prepared the terrified teenager for surgery. A sterile, uniformed staff surrounded him. An abrupt, harried anesthesiologist put Terry to sleep. The surgeon quickly removed the bullet.

"Tag it and bag it," he said.

The operation was an immediate success, saving Terry's mobility. At that moment Terry learned how precious and tenuous life could be. Where darkness and violence seemed to dominate, Terry survived, raised animals, and looked out for his siblings. He developed a warrior's understanding of battle and its potentially devastating consequences. He soon faced a turning point in a growing rock 'n' roll era.

Terry missed his impounded motorcycle, but Harry wouldn't let the young man fool with his collection of Indians. "I saved every nickel, dime, and quarter I made," Terry said, "and started to build another motorcycle piece by piece."

He bought a rigid 1950s Panhead frame from the monster San Gabriel Valley H-D dealership, Laidlaw's, and a friend told him of a guy in the Devil's Disciples who straightened and raked frames in El Monte. For $50, he had his frame checked and altered.

He stashed '51 chopper parts at his stepbrother Eddie's pad. From some struggling members of the Chosen Few he bought a 61-inch Panhead engine for $100, plus a transmission. He purchased parts weekly and tried to figure out how they fit together.

Alma loaded Terry up in her '59 Ford station wagon and hauled him to the old, dilapidated El Monte continuation campus next to the football field every Saturday, religiously. He crawled out of the Ford, said his goodbyes, and watched the long, tan wagon pull away. He walked to the front door of the dour-looking building and studied the stained granite front steps guarded by a large, foreboding, concrete lion.

To Terry, the gloomy, ominous building represented nothing but structure and confinement. Terry strolled briskly through the polished linoleum halls and straight out the back door, crossed the football field, and exited the property through the chain-link gate. He crawled into Harry's waiting '59 Ford pickup and they cut a dusty trail to another studio gig. He never graduated from high school, and Alma went nuts when she found out.

Members of a couple of local motorcycle clubs, the Coffin Cheaters and the Henchmen, helped Terry obtain a 17-inch front wheel with no front brake.

"It kept spitting bearings," Terry said.

After four months of tinkering and installing a 10-inch-over Wide Glide front fork, Terry was once more in the wind. He rode to Harry's place, but Harry wasn't impressed.

"You can't make money with one of those," Harry said. "You can't bulldog it, can't stand on the seat and ride in circles, and you can't jump it." It was a chopper, and choppers belonged to a special, outcast world of wild young men who didn't fit in, didn't want social structure, and didn't give a shit about doing tricks on motorcycles.

Terry hung out at the Tasty Freeze, trying to meet girls in tight-fitting Levi's and bobby socks and learning that choppers didn't mesh with the streets or culture of Los Angeles. Over the next two years he collected more than seventy-four tickets that ran the gamut from having no mirror, license, or horn, to leaking oil, to having loud pipes, to riding a flat-out unsafe motorcycle. He learned the streets of Los Angeles and started to hang out way too late at Richey's Café on Garvey, the main boulevard in El Monte, just one of the concrete umbilical cords that held Los Angeles together.

After four months of tinkering and installing a 10-inch-over Wide Glide front fork, Terry was once more in the wind.

Harry never punished or abused Terry for his teenage antics but initiated prankster tactics to discipline the seventeen-year-old when he stepped out of line.

"He tried pulling the coil wire on my '56 Crown Victoria," Terry said. One day when he was out too late, Harry jacked up the rear of Terry's car so when Terry hustled to make it to work on time, the wheels spun helplessly in the air. Harry made his point.

Harry proved relentless in his quest to keep Terry out of trouble. He constantly took knives away from Terry. "Let me see that," Harry would say, and Terry always offered up his hot new, razor-sharp blade.

"I'd never see it again," Terry said.

In 1965, Terry hooked up with the wildest woman of his life. One night he parked his Panhead out front of Richey's, the local after-hours coffee shop. He strolled in, winked at Corky, the tall, hot waitress, and made his way to the juke box at the end of the counter, opposite the Textolite and chrome booths. As he punched in a couple of new Elvis tunes, a big brute of a man made a comment and he turned to face him and the cute bubbly babe at his side.

"I'm going to shove that taco up your ass, punk," Terry said, and the fight ensued. He yanked the big man out of the booth and kicked him out the front door of Richey's. But there was something captivating about the girl beside the bruiser.

The girl would become the second unruly woman to enter Terry's life. Like his mother, this wavy-haired blonde bombshell, Tekla, hated motorcycles. She hated chopper riders in particular. They couldn't be tamed, and that drove the nest-bound woman nuts. But there was a chemical attraction. The next night she parked her curvaceous form in a booth at Richey's to wait for the wavy-haired Terry when he rolled in from work at the studios. They hooked up like two charged magnets and became as connected as his Panhead engine was to its traditional 4-speed transmission.

> Like his mother, this wavy-haired blonde bombshell, Tekla, hated motorcycles. She hated chopper riders in particular.

Tekla's mother raised three girls and two boys on her own. One of Tekla's sisters ultimately became Miss Palm Springs. They were a hot-looking bunch. Tekla's mother supported the family by working as a hotel maid in southern California after she'd left her husband, the legendary Big Ed Thompson.

"I never met him," Terry said of Thompson. "I spoke to him once, but it wasn't good."

Big Ed owned an antique shop in Sonora, California, a small town of around 4,500 people located almost dead-center in the state. Sonora was founded by Mexican miners during the California Gold Rush. Big Ed was a giant of a man who was known to clear the town of rowdy bikers armed only with a two-by-four.

"I saw him once from afar," Terry said of Big Ed. A waitress in a diner pointed out the big man. "You ain't seen nothin' until you see big Ed Thompson," she told Terry.

Apparently she was right, because according to Terry, "When the waitress pointed him out, I took one look and left."

Terry would never forget meeting Tekla's chain-smoking mom in their tiny El Monte bungalow.

"I knocked on the door and heard a clamor, and a squawking woman," Terry said.

"He better be good-looking," Tekla's mom hollered as she yanked open the door. Like Tekla she was a wild woman, unruly and violent.

The relationship was stormy from the start. Terry was hardly Beaver Cleaver himself, and he instigated more than one violent encounter with Tekla. Take the time he started dating a short blonde named Judy, who lived in one of the bungalows next to the one in which Tekla's mother lived. Things went fine, at least until Tekla found out.

"It was on and crankin'," Terry said. Tekla barreled out through the front door of their bungalow with her mom in tow, dragged Judy into the front yard, and beat her unmercifully.

"I should have learned," Terry said. "If she had said she was going to shoot someone, you could bet on it."

Terry got his first real taste of the raucous wickedness this woman was capable of when he told her he wouldn't marry her. She came unglued and shot up his car with a 30-30 Winchester carbine. In 1966 Terry buckled to Tekla's marriage desires and they slipped across the border into Tijuana for an impromptu, illegal transaction.

An unrelenting, wild mare of a woman had snagged Terry and there was no way out. He couldn't leave her, couldn't run. She needed to feel the warm success of childbirth, and he was the unsuspecting missionary. In 1967, with Tekla pregnant, Terry relented once more and they were married on the U.S. side of the border.

"Terry himself overreacted when he discovered Tekla with another guy. "I got a call from my brother, who was at Denny's," he said.

Terry rode into the parking lot, straight pipes blaring. He stormed the interior, where he spotted the sandy-blonde Tekla sitting across from a straight-looking, nondescript young

> Tekla barreled out through the front door of their bungalow with her mom in tow, dragged Judy into the front yard, and beat her unmercifully.

Hispanic man. Terry didn't bother to ask questions or study body language, his usual warrior security measures. He grabbed the short-haired kid, dragged him from the booth, and started to pound on him.

The kid broke free and darted from the restaurant.

"He just gave me a lift from Riverside!" Tekla shouted at Terry. "There's nothing going on!"

"Don't ever bring a boyfriend into my town," Terry responded. Tekla never brought another man into El Monte again.

Terry's life was burning along, and biker movies would add flame to his fire. Novelist Hunter S. Thompson's biographical book *Hells Angels* shot up the best-seller charts in the summer of 1966. Director Roger Corman was impressed with the *Life* magazine image of a menacing pack of choppers rolling into a California cemetery for the funeral of a dead biker. He worked with screenplay writer Charles Griffith to create the biker movie, *Wild Angels*, with the cooperation of Columbia and American International studios.

The next year Terry worked on the Anthony Lanza biker movie *Glory Stompers*, starring Dennis Hopper and Jody McCrea. Terry worked with members of the Gypsy Jokers during the filming in an isolated woods in the San Fernando Valley. In the film the character Chino and his fictitious rebel motorcycle gang, The Black Souls, capture Darryl, leader of a rival gang called The Glory Stompers, and Darryl's girlfriend, Chris. One of the Black Souls attempts to rape Chris, and Chino beats up Darryl. Subsequently, the whole gang jumps Darryl, leaves him for dead, and rides like mad wolves for a border town to sell Chris to Mexican white slavers. In the meantime, Chino's advances toward Chris infuriated Jo Ann, his "momma." A disillusioned former Glory Stomper named Smiley, now traveling alone, happens upon the wounded Darryl, and together they set out to rescue Chris.

"I taught Dennis Hopper how to ride a jockey shift," Terry said. "He was difficult to teach when he was stoned, and he was stoned all the time."

Terry's life was rockin'. Aretha Franklin dominated the airwaves with her first soul record, "Respect," ultimately becoming the most popular female singer in rock history. Together with Terry for just two years, Tekla was already pregnant with their second child.

"Our first daughter died at birth," Terry said. "I rushed Tekla to the hospital when her water broke and she went into labor, but something went wrong."

Tekla was a different woman, hardened and scared, when their only son, Terry Jr., was born.

Meanwhile Terry dodged cops, doing his best to avoid adding to his collection of infractions. One summer day when his newborn son was just a week old, Terry spotted another rider broken down on Garvey Boulevard as he rolled toward work. With the warm Southern California sun on his back, the rumbling Harley singing in one ear and a new Temptations R&B tune warming the other, he stopped to help the rider. Gypsy, the broke-down biker was a young member of the Gypsy Jokers, riding an old tin-can Harley Panhead. Terry pulled over on the sidewalk. The long-haired outlaw was mechanically lost, his scooter a mass of rusting sheet metal and his engine covered in oil.

"The bike was a mess," Terry said, "and I noticed that this scrawny biker wore a number of leather-sheathed knives. Some were like swords."

He checked the points on the Harley. They were closed, which shut off the fire to his coil and ultimately the sparkplugs. Terry adjusted them with the back of a matchbook, which was approximately .015-inch (the point gap called for .022), and the bike fired to life.

A cop spotted the two wild youngsters in downtown El Monte and pulled them over. He immediately started to write Terry another ticket. He clearly didn't like bikers and wrote him up for leaking oil on the sidewalk, parking on the sidewalk, heading the wrong direction, and operating an unsafe vehicle. Terry's second motorcycle was towed away.

"I taught Dennis Hopper how to ride a jockey shift," Terry said. "He was difficult to teach when he was stoned, and he was stoned all the time."

Terry's outstanding tickets won him a quick trip to jail, even though he complained profusely that he just had a son and was trying to get to work. After spending several hours in a holding cell, he was thrust in front of the judge, who looked at Terry's record with dismay.

"It's a miracle you are still on the streets," he said. "I'm sentencing you to thirty days, and you'll never see that bike again."

"I just had a son," Terry said.

"Do whatever time you can, and we'll take care of the rest, but don't ever come before me again, or I'll give you a year in County."

It was an era of racial unrest that exploded on the streets of Los Angeles. On August 11, 1965, the Watts neighborhood in Los Angeles experienced a complete social breakdown, devolving into a post-apocalyptic landscape of rioting and mob rule. The eruption of violence began when Lee Minikus, a California Highway Patrol motorcycle officer, pulled over Marquette Frye, an African American. Minikus believed Frye, whom he had observed driving erratically, was drunk. Frye failed to pass field sobriety tests, including walking a straight line and touching his nose, so Minikus arrested him.

The situation escalated when Minikus refused to let Frye's brother, Ronald, drive Frye's car home and radioed for it to be impounded. Frye's mother intervened and the situation heated up. As events escalated, the crowd of onlookers grew from dozens to hundreds. As more police arrived, the mob became violent, throwing rocks and other objects while shouting at the police officers. Then all hell broke loose. The police arrested both of the Frye brothers as well as their mother, but it was too late to prevent the city from going up in flames.

Though the riots began in August, they were the result of much more than just the arrest of the Frye family. Racial tension had grown so thick it was almost visible. The riots that began on August 11 had been building steam for a long time. Investigations into the riots placed the blame on poverty, inequality, racial discrimination, and the passage in November 1964 of Proposition 14, which overturned a law that established equality of opportunity for black home buyers. Regardless the cause, the events of August 11 drove people to the breaking point. Violence spilled onto the streets and Watts burned for four days.

For the better part of a week, society completely broke down. Residents looted stores, vandalized property, and seriously threatened the security of the city. Many people engaged in fights with police, blocked the firemen of the Los Angeles Fire Department from performing their duties, and even beat white motorists. Others took advantage of the riot and broke into stores, stealing whatever they could and setting the stores themselves on fire.

They wanted to kill us all during the LA race riots.

Los Angeles Police Chief William Parker also fueled the radicalized tension that caused the explosion of violence by publicly labeling the people involved in the riots as "monkeys in the zoo."

Eventually the National Guard cordoned off a vast region of South Los Angeles from Alameda Street to Crenshaw Boulevard, and from just south of the Santa Monica Freeway to Rosecrans Avenue, finally bringing the situation under control. Overall, an estimated $40 million in damage was caused as almost 1,000 buildings were damaged or destroyed. Most of the physical damage was confined to white-owned businesses that were said to have caused resentment in the neighborhood due to perceived unfairness. Thirty-four people died, twenty-five of them black, and an estimated 1,000 more were injured.

"They wanted to kill us all during the LA race riots," Terry said.

Martha and The Vandellas' "Dancing in the Streets" was used as a rallying cry when the racial riots ignited. Los Angeles disc jockey The Magnificent Montague's slogan, "Burn Baby Burn," took on a new meaning as the streets of Los Angeles went up in flames. Shit was happening fast in Southern California.

Terry did twenty-five days of his thirty-day sentence and returned home. It was not a good time for a white boy to be locked up among extremely angry black men, and it wasn't an experience Terry cared to repeat. He never got a traffic warrant again. ☠

A New Southern California Outlaw Patch Kicked Off in 1965

THE WORD "VAGO" IS SHORT FOR "VAGABOND," a hell-raiser or trouble-maker. In 1965 a group of men with the unlikely names of Berdoo Moose, Poodle, J.R., Psycho, Whitey, Sugar Bear, and Hall kicked off the Vagos Motorcycle Club. They were just boys running wild in the streets of San Bernardino, the home of the Hells Angels (established in 1948). Poodle had been a member of the Mescaleros, a local motorcycle club, but the other Mescaleros decided Poodle was a psycho and kicked him out of the club.

"Fuck you," he told the members who pulled his patch. "I'm going to start a bigger, nastier club." He stormed out of the clubhouse and launched the Vagos.

A wild, uncontrolled, turbulent era was just about to begin. Poodle and his brothers didn't know what they were getting into. The mid-1960s proved a tipping point for America and its people. Alan Freed, who coined the term "rock 'n' roll" and introduced it to white America a decade earlier, died in 1965 of alcoholism at age forty-four,

Most clubs have abolished the wearing of any club patch by women. The Vagos is one of the few clubs keeping the old "Property of . . . " tradition alive. At least you know who not to mess with.

broke and forgotten. Protest-rock erupted on American radio that same year, focusing on timely topics such as the escalating war in Vietnam ("Eve of Destruction," by Barry McGuire), the civil rights battles in America ("People Get Ready," by the Impressions), and a general rebellion against authority as portrayed in any number of songs, such as the Rolling Stones surly number one hit, "Satisfaction."

Over the next decade what started out as fun became serious business, business that many chopper-riding motorcycle maniacs didn't survive. The parties turned into violent blood baths fueled by mind-altering drugs. Meanwhile, Terry struggled with life as a family man, balancing the demands of an irrepressible broad and his first son, who meant everything to him. Tekla was the consummate evil nester. She wanted everything—control, a comfortable home, and a secure family. The more Terry wandered, the more she fought him.

> "The parties turned into violent blood baths fueled by mind-altering drugs."

His brother, Eddie, started to hang around clubs and became a member of the Dirty Dozen in Los Angeles, which had nothing to do with the Arizona-based, one-percenter organization of the same name.

Initially, motorcycle clubs consisted of guys looking for wild times aboard glistening choppers. They avoided organization, structure, and rules, but running wild in the streets didn't last. Territorial boundaries were drawn, patches were pulled, club business became mired with rules, and the almighty buck got involved.

Eddie's psyche was laced with a serious violent streak that manifested itself as meanness toward women. A brother gave the stout, five-foot nine-inch, sandy-blonde, mustachioed biker with no tattoos the nickname "Parts." He started to run with the Vikings, the Coffin Cheaters, the Hangmen, the Henchmen, Satan's Slaves, and the Vagos from Berdoo. The Vagos began with the Berdoo chapter and then branched out. First they started a small chapter in the high desert town of Victorville, followed by another in Monterey Park, a suburb of Los Angeles.

He started to run with the Vikings, the Coffin Cheaters, the Hangmen, the Henchmen, Satan's Slaves, and the Vagos from Berdoo.

In 1967, another group sprung out of the streets of West Covina, the 13th Rank. They tried to make a name for themselves. During a party, they picked up Champ, a Vietnam vet and a well-known young member of the Dirty Dozen, from the streets of El Monte. The kid was partially disabled, and everyone in town knew him. The Rank members got drunk and high, then beat the kid half to death. They dumped him out of the back of a pickup on the freeway. His leg braces saved his life when he crashed onto the unforgiving asphalt at more than 60 miles per hour.

Parts knew Champ. The incident infuriated him, as well as members of the Vagos, the Sabers, and the Dirty Dozen. He hauled representatives of all the small LA-based clubs to a Vagos meeting and proposed creating a San Gabriel chapter of the Vagos. The Vagos approved the chapter and their ranks began to grow. That one night expanded their membership by 125. The new troops set out to avenge Champ's beating and the shit began to fly.

"They kicked down doors and kicked ass," Terry said.

Parts was trouble, but he was always on hand for Terry and the club. Terry fought Parts, his most trusted stepbrother, three times. "I could never win—he hit like a sledgehammer—but we fought any-way," Terry said, "usually over women." Parts was built solid inside and out. He was always a gangster, stealing cars and dealing drugs, getting hooked on coke in the process. Terry and Parts first fight revolved around Parts's first marriage to Terry's blood sister, Sandy.

"That didn't go down well. I knew it would mean trouble." Parts had two boys with Sandy before the relationship unraveled.

Around that time, James Brown made an abrupt shift from pure soul to a rhythm-based new invention of his own making called funk with the hits, "Papa's Got A Brand New Bag," and, "I Got You." Funk, which was more frantic and explosive than traditional rhythm and blues, better captured the atmosphere that permeated the era.

Terry avoided clubs at his young age and no longer owned a motorcycle after the last one was impounded. "Tekla hated motorcycles and despised club guys even more," Terry said. His old lady might have hated the club life, but Terry could feel a shift welling in his consciousness.

Parts messed around with a number of women, and one turned on him when she discovered that she wasn't the only one coupled with the tough guy. She called the cops and filed kidnapping charges. The next night, Parts was pulled over on his way to the Bunny Run, a biker bar on the edge of town. He was rousted by LA County sheriffs and hauled to lock-up. He called Terry from jail.

Terry drove out to the Bunny Run, a rundown biker bar in a strip mall. It had a jail cell nailed to the back of the simple stucco structure where they tossed drunks to sleep it off. The Bunny Run was anything but a friendly joint. Nobody came to the Run unless they knew someone, or could box their way into the seedy saloon. Terry knew a few of the brothers and sought out Butch, the young president with a constant smile.

"What are you going to do about Parts?" Terry asked.

"Nothing," Butch said. "It wasn't club business."

Terry left the bar disgruntled, mustered the cash, and bailed Parts out, but the notion of club brothers not backing a brother ate at him.

"I didn't get it," Terry said somberly. "My brother was in jail, and the club wasn't doing anything, no bail, no attorney, nothing. So I went to find out why."

Terry took off work and attended Parts's hearing in downtown Pomona. He cleaned up, dressed the part of a courtroom citizen, and arrived at the court on time. He was twenty-four years old, with long thick hair and a small frame. The judge and bailiff warily eyed the surly club members as they swaggered into court, unruly, disrespectful, and uncontrollable. The year was 1972, the height of the drug revolution. Wearing shredded Levi's jackets, greasy denim pants, and Vagos patches, they raised quite a stink, which didn't much help Parts's cause.

The bikers in the courtroom were just young outlaws passing from one party to the next. Terry was focused on a singular goal, getting his brother out of jail. He had no respect for the lawless club members and showed it in his demeanor. Finally, one of the members confronted the swaggering young loner.

"What's your problem?" a gruff biker demanded, eyeing Terry's direct countenance. It was One-Eyed Willie, a Charles Manson-type character with one eye and a notoriously evil spirit. Even though he stood less than five feet tall, he didn't care if you were a monster or armed to the teeth. He was dead serious and dead ready for anything.

"That's my brother," Terry fired back. "And he's in your club. What the hell are you doing to help?"

He stared into the eyes of the small man.

"Got a lawyer? Any bail money? I'm going to need some assistance getting him out," Terry said, continuing his eyeball-to-eyeball assessment of the nefarious man.

The patch-holder looked away from Terry's unblinking gaze, a sign of weakness. "We don't have shit," he admitted.

Looking back at it today, Terry says, "That was bullshit," referring to the club's resources, or rather lack of resources for helping out a brother in need. Terry took matters into his own hands and raised $1,700 to hire the attorney. Finally the attorney revealed the jealous girlfriend's intentions. The judge cut Parts loose, and Terry had impressed One-Eyed Willie.

Two weeks after his brother was released, Terry began to hang around the motley crew of Vagos. He sensed an organizational need within the club, and although he was devoted to his son, his wife was pushing all the wrong buttons.

Terry found himself as conflicted as society itself. Times were changing, but a lot of old-fashioned notions still held sway. This was apparent on January 1, 1972, when Three Dog Night became the first rock band to appear on a float in the Tournament of Roses New Year's Parade, in Pasadena, California, while Lawrence Welk was still the Grand Marshal of the parade. 🕱

A New Member:
Terry the Tramp

TERRY'S IMPRESSION OF THE VAGOS wasn't healthy after his brother's trial. "They were young, broke-dick dogs," Terry said.

There was little organization. Dues were two bucks a week, so the club's coffers were limited. Even though Terry wasn't a member of the club, the power vacuum within the organization sucked him in. Right away he began to right the ship, creating a structure that would act as a safety net for the club brothers should they find themselves in a situation like the one Parts found himself in. He introduced them to Joe Barnum, a bail bondsman. The relationship proved fruitful and Barnum supported the Vagos for the next thirty years, teaching them a few tricks along the way. At one time Joe was thrust into the unenviable position of having to bail out 100 members after a statewide bust.

"Collecting money was like pulling teeth," Terry recalled.

Terry had no intention of joining a club until he started working in a small Triumph shop, Bud's Custom Cycles, to augment his floundering studio income. That set Tekla off for the final time.

"I rode a Triumph Bonneville home one night," Terry said. "She went nuts and ran off. She said, 'Fuck you and motorcycles,' and split."

Terry was left to raise his young son alone. In his rambunctious way Terry tried to be a responsible, single dad and create a stable atmosphere, and ultimately he came to one disheartening conclusion. He couldn't bring girls home.

"I didn't want Terry Jr. to think any of these broads were his mom," Terry said. Besides there was always the threat of the wild woman—Tekla—showing up, or of club demands interfering.

His sister watched Terry Jr., who was also called "Terry the Wall" or "Boomer," while Terry started to hang out with other bikers. He bought a rat Triumph twin for $600 from a Vago named Whitey, who was going to jail and needed money for a lawyer. Terry started to ride with Butch, Jerry the Jew, and Prophet, all Vagos.

The brothers learned a lesson in brotherhood and courtroom antics, and they were showing respect.

"If I went to work and Tekla showed up at home, she'd toss my Triumph parts in the gutter," Terry said. "I came home and found my parts up and down the street in the storm drain."

One night while partying at Hollywood East, Terry got drunk and was arrested for public drunkenness. The next morning, the young biker was hauled into court to face a judge.

"I looked out at the courtroom and there they were: Butch, Jerry the Jew, and Prophet," Terry said. They were respectful and prepared. "That touched a chord with me."

For the first time in his life, his leadership made a difference. The brothers learned a lesson in brotherhood and courtroom antics, and they were showing respect. He finally became a prospect and started the wild rigors of the round-the-clock probation period.

It was another learning period for the brothers on both sides of the fence, the members and prospective members.

"A member called me Little Parts," Terry said, "but after a while, the nickname lost its appeal. I told him to knock it off."

That led to a fight with Deacon, a bad-ass member of the Monterey chapter. He was a store-bought reverend, courtesy of an ad in the back of *Rolling Stone* magazine, and a mean motherfucker. The Monterey chapter was tough.

"I was always being tested against the Monterey chapter guys." Terry constantly had to rely on his fists to settle these tests. "For two years, I rode around with broken hands." Terry had to watch his back twenty-four hours a day.

"I learned that a fight was just a fight, and not to carry a grudge." Learning not to harbor any bitterness did not come naturally or easily for Terry, as was apparent when an A Val Bear—a member of the A Val chapter of the club—caught Terry at a party and gave him an assignment that didn't sit especially well with Terry.

"Here's a rag—clean all the spokes on my bike," he demanded. For six months, Terry endured various levels of prospect abuse. In the process One-Eyed Willie gave him the nickname Terry the Tramp.

"There was a prospect member code within the member ranks," Terry said. "You didn't ask any prospect to do anything you wouldn't do."

The prospect period took on a blue-collar, motorcycle-mechanical, frat boys' initiation essence, but with a violent edge fueled by wild chopper runs and all-night drunken nightmares. Being a prospect meant looking after brothers who were falling down drunk. It also meant keeping your mouth shut when a citizen was getting his ass kicked or when a brother slapped around a chick behind a Los Angeles bar.

Some of the brothers were regular, working, blue-collar guys. Others were quiet types until too much tequila melted brain cells and they discovered rampant bravery behind a dozen shots. Terry played the game, riding behind his San Gabriel pack from party to clubhouse.

Terry stood the test of probation successfully, only to have his struggling motorcycle explode the day before he would be voted on for membership.

Butch, the club president, warned him, "If you expect to become a member, that motorcycle better be running before the meeting tomorrow night."

Butch, the club president, warned him, "If you expect to become a member, that motorcycle better be running before the meeting tomorrow night."

Terry worked on the old Triumph all night and the next day. He rode to the meeting with his hands still coated with the grease of his labors.

Prospects were required to stand outside of the meeting place and guard the perimeter like junior soldiers on watch. They were only allowed to attend the meeting unless called upon. The members sat on stools and milk crates surrounding a partially assembled motorcycle project in the center of the room. They handled the meeting with sloppy Roberts' Rules of Order.

Standing just five-feet, eight-inches tall, Butch, the president, wasn't a big man and didn't have a beard or the usual biker long hair. He was a pipe fitter and got pissed off when he drank. He could be fearsome when he put his mind to it.

One night in a canyon bar, Butch witnessed a tall bean-pole of a guy slapping a girl, trying to force her to be a turn-out, that is, to be raped by various members. Butch had had enough to drink that night, and although he wasn't a great fighter, he beat the skinny son of a bitch senseless and took the girl. She was pregnant and when the child was born with Down syndrome, he looked after both her and the child. They built a home together and had three more children.

Butch called Terry into the meeting and told him they were about to consider him for full membership.

While Terry prospected with the Vagos he also worked two jobs and raised a son as a single dad. He was fed up with the petty bullshit, and that night at the meeting in Butch's garage, he drew a line in the El Monte dirt.

"I was thinking about turning in my shit," Terry said. He had been partying all over Los Angeles for three days without any sleep. He had been disrespected by a couple of members, and he was rapidly losing his frayed patience.

"Either vote for me or I'm out of here," he demanded.

They took a vote and while standing on the greasy concrete floor of a Rosemead garage he became a member of the Vagos MC.

This was in 1971, just a year after the movie *Easy Rider*, was released, starring Dennis Hopper, Peter Fonda, and Jack Nicholson.

"Let"s have a party," One-Eyed Willie said.

"Bullshit," Terry said, "I don't have time for a party. I've got business to take care of."

He rode directly out to Acton, on the edge of the desert, and found the dusty road where A Val Bear lived. He had watched Bear force his girlfriend to give him head in front of other members at a bar and the sight never left him. He knocked on the old door of the small ranch style home and when no one answered, he kicked in the door, stormed into the house, and found Bear sprawled out in a comfortable easy chair. Terry pounded him unmercifully, pulled his patch, and rode back to El Monte to report it to his president.

"I was tired of all the fighting, the trickbags, and bullshit," Terry said. "This bastard had to go."

A Val Bear wasn't the only member to feel Terry's wrath. He hunted down another member, a scraggly haired, thin heroin addict and bitched-slapped him. "He was only brave when ten brothers were around," Terry said.

Ten days later, his president took him aside again.

"You have thirty days to shit-can that Triumph and get a Harley," he warned. Terry sold the feeble British ride within a week.

He was at a party when a girl told a story of a Harley Panhead. It was owned by her brother, who left for Vietnam and never returned. Her father never sold the bike. It remained in the family garage. Terry asked if he would like to sell it and how much.

"How about $500?" she said.

"Hell, yes," Terry responded, and they drove to Huntington Beach to find the bike under a growing pile of collected newspapers. The bone-stock 1957 Panhead had sat collecting moisture from the nearby Pacific Ocean and dust from the newspapers for nearly a decade. It was green with mold and rusty, but he uncovered it and hauled it home.

He was just getting the hang of the classic Panhead, produced during the last year of that historic engine, when Parts was arrested for murder.

> ## Terry pounded him unmercifully, pulled his patch, and rode back to El Monte to report it to his president.

"I sold the Panhead to a Vago named Huey to help with the bail," Terry said. "We didn't have any money for an attorney, so they assigned Parts a black public defender. I knew the club brothers wouldn't like the public defender, but I convinced them to give him a shot. I rode Parts's bike while he was in jail."

It was a manslaughter beef but Parts tried to run, so the cops jacked up the charge to murder. The public defender presented a compelling case and Parts was released once more, but Terry lost another motorcycle.

A few months into membership, Terry considered leaving the club. He enjoyed hanging with Butch, who worked constantly, and Jerry the Jew, a well-educated string bean of a man who owned a couple of bars.

"Jerry joked a lot, laughed and kidded," Terry said. "He carried an oriental spoon and always went after the potato salad at any party."

But the bullshit, the constant fights, and the slovenly members depressed him. Terry had a small home with his son, and he wanted it kept separate from the club.

"Some people lived like pigs," Terry said and he didn't want it rubbing off on him or his son. "How can folks live like this?" It turned his stomach.

Jerry was a contradiction to many of the members. He fell in love with a young hippy and bought her a home. He lived a comfortable, sedate, middle-class life at home during the week, and on the weekends he partied with the club. Then one Saturday he rode into a San Gabriel Valley Shell gas station with his love on the back of his long chopper. A truck rear-ended the narrow, chromed out Harley chopper, killing his girl instantly. It crushed Jerry and he was never the same. He got hooked on drugs and dropped dead a few years later.

Terry worked a couple of jobs at the studios, watched out for his son, and then met a new girl, a dark-haired Italian with a warm heart, Rosemary Cosintino. He called her Sheila.

Sheila, a young, knockout Denny's waitress, got to know Terry on the nights he held court there over coffee and greasy food. She was just nineteen when she met the twenty-seven-year-old wild man, who led a handful of notorious outlaws into the restaurant every night.

A truck rear-ended the narrow, chromed out Harley chopper, killing his girl instantly.

One Friday night Sheila asked to hang with the guys and ended up straddling Terry's wild chopper for an even wilder night ride to party at the Hut in Pasadena. Sheila's sister climbed on another green chopper and followed.

"I recommended that they pass," Terry said, "but she wanted to come."

They tore north on the old concrete 110 freeway, the oldest winding freeway in the country, into Pasadena. It was just another crazed night of drinking, pushing folks around and riding like madmen. On their way back into El Monte, swerving across freeway lanes and raising hell, they were followed and pulled over by a couple of Los Angeles sheriffs.

"Tramp, pull your bike over to the emergency lane," the cop barked from his patrol car speaker. Once off the freeway, one officer gave them a ride in his black and white to the Denny's on Peck Road, while the other straddled and rode Terry's bike.

"Don't let him leave here until he sobers up," the cop told Sheila.

The cop who rode Terry's bike into the parking lot took the key to Sheila. She never asked to attend a Vago gathering again.

Sheila helped Terry with his young son and watched after his home while he roamed the streets with the Vagos, tearing up bars and beating riders out of their motorcycles.

Tekla was a wild, unruly woman and a harsh mother who didn't give an inch of slack to anyone, and never received a break. She stayed in school and graduated from a nursing program. Pam was a bouncing child of the Hollywood scene and the hippy generation, full of financial recourses and the desire to be one with nature, nurturing animals and doing her own thing. Sheila was all soft curves with a warm heart, a family desire, and instructions to pray. "She was deeply religious,"

Sheila was all soft curves, a warm heart, and a family desire, and instructions to pray.

Terry said, "and she wanted me to pray a lot." She would do anything for Terry.

Sheila came from a close-knit family. Her dad drove a bus and raised his family using old-fashioned values. Her mother was always respectful, even when Sheila brought a grubby biker around. Her older brother Jim worked for Disney Studios, and her other brother Mike was an architect but faced constant health issues. Her sister Liz was a long-haul truck driver with her husband, but he had a massive heart attack and died.

Sheila's life was one of deep religious faith and stability, yet she reached into the treacherous life of an outlaw and dabbled in the risky waters. Sheila and Terry played together for a few years, but she didn't find a home in the outlaw lifestyle. She drifted into another job working as a waitress at a steakhouse, where she met a band leader and married.

"I met him once over too many drinks," Terry said. "When the conversation shifted to Sheila we had to part ways before trouble erupted. He was a decent guy."

The marriage lasted less than a year before she returned to live with her folks and date Terry.

"We started to get close again in the early eighties," Terry said, "but I took her to Vegas and that broke the bond." At that time Terry was the special effects coordinator on a Matt Cimber-directed film, *Fake Out*, with Telly Savalas, Desi Arnaz Jr., and Pia Zadora. The party atmosphere was hot and heavy.

At first blush Sheila enjoyed the ride, enjoyed hanging with the stars.

"She was offered a bit part in the movie," Terry said. "All the guys wanted a piece of her." Standing five-feet, eight-inches, with all the right curves perfectly located on her voluptuous body, Sheila was a happy-go-lucky knockout, always neatly dressed in form-fitting Levi's, carefully color-coordinated.

While Terry worked during the day, Sheila watched Terry Jr., but as the weeks rolled on Terry found the blackjack tables mesmerizing.

All-night gambling sessions and parties rocked every neon-lit Vegas evening, and the crew, including the director, couldn't keep their eyes—and sometimes their hands—off Sheila.

"I stepped in one time," Terry said, "and put a stop to the hanky panky." Sheila was having fun, but the lifestyle didn't fit her family-oriented, religious-based upbringing. One too many late nights at the blackjack tables and Sheila loaded up Terry Jr. and returned to the city.

Throughout this time Terry was constantly on the edge of leaving the club. There were incessant arrests for bullshit offenses and the brothers couldn't build homes or security if they had to sell all their shit to bail out other brothers constantly.

One night a member announced at a meeting that if he rode to any brother's pad and needed a part, he would take it.

"I told him to come on over," Terry said. "If he touched any of my shit I'd kick his ass."

Terry was learning the ways of the outlaw, the streets, and the legal community at break-neck speed. He was busted for an unsafe vehicle violation in Temple City, California, by the Los Angeles sheriffs in 1972. He was required to ride his chopper to court, where he met a young rookie attorney named Francis "Frank" Gately, who became a Rio Hondo judge and a life-long friend and confidant. Gately proved almost as colorful as any member of the Vagos. When he retired from the Los Angeles Superior Court in 2008 because, in his own words, "time's a-footin'," he said that his proudest accomplishment was "saving the western world." When the Berlin Wall fell on the very same day that he was appointed to the old Rio Hondo Municipal Court, Gately said, "Once the Commies heard I was judge, they surrendered."

"Frank asked me to give him a ride to prove my bike was safe," Terry said. "I did, and he was convinced." ☠

A New Panhead and
Terry's First Club Run

TERRY HAD TO BUILD ANOTHER MOTORCYCLE, so he bought a basket case and started to build it in the bedroom of his ground-floor apartment. He did this on top of working two jobs, looking after his son, and trying to build a relationship with the lovely Sheila, all the while flying his Vago patch and being an honorable club brother. This, of course, meant that he honored the code of the one-percenter by having a running motorcycle.

Another obstacle to his growing love for Sheila was Tekla, who entered his life like a fiery tornado from time to time, took his son, threw his motorcycle parts in the gutter, and disrupted every relationship in his life. His relationship with Tekla wasn't all bad, Terry recalled. "She was there for me on more than one occasion."

Sheila was the polar opposite of Tekla. She swept into his life like warm sunlight on a summer morning.

J. J., an outstanding thirty-five-year member of the San Gabriel Chapter of the Vagos, in 1990 at Terry the Tramp's wedding at Pam's Grass Valley, California, ranch.

Terry had to build another motorcycle, so he bought a basket case and started to build it in the bedroom of his ground-floor apartment.

But Terry wasn't surprised when Sheila began to move away from him. With the kind of life he led, something had to give, and that something was his relationship with Sheila.

"I couldn't give her the kind of home she deserved," Terry said. "I had to let her go."

"She was way too good for me," Terry said. They parted ways but always remained friends, even after she married someone else and had one boy and twin girls. "She was drop-dead gorgeous and treated my son as if he was one of her children."

The new bike started its life as a mid-1950s, 74-cubic-inch big twin, though there wasn't much of the original bike left when Terry finished with it. Dick Latsky of Atlas Precision modified the frame and built the coffin gas tank, the oil bucket, and the tall sissy bar.

Dick and Peggy Latsky, the owners of Atlas Precision /Pro Magnum, successfully designed and built custom frames to accept Harley-Davidson motorcycle engines starting in 1967. Dick's talents and accomplishments were known and recognized throughout the Harley-Davidson motorcycle industry.

Dick put years of talent and study into the design, engineering, and manufacture of all Atlas chassis components. Atlas frames were built from the finest material. All mounts and brackets were carefully laser-cut and machined from billet steel. Each tube was bent and machined to an exact fit, and all completed components were carefully assembled and heli-arc (TIG) welded in precision fixtures.

Terry molded the Atlas-modified frame, filling his bedroom with Bondo dust and shavings as he filed and shaped each frame contour. Prophet painted the frame and sheet metal a collage of psychedelic colors. Terry carefully installed chromed high bars, short drag pipes, a custom seat, but never a front brake. What began as a chromed-out, 20-over Wide Glide Panhead ultimately received a Shovelhead top end, and eventually a complete electric-start stroker

Shovel engine. This scooter in various permutations stuck with Terry for three decades.

When the multicolored, wild-eyed chopper was completed in 1973, Terry couldn't maneuver the long, gangly motorcycle out of his apartment. With the help of a brother, he tore a hole in the stucco and stud wall leading into the living room with sledgehammers and pry bars. They carefully rolled the chromed-out chopper to glistening freedom in the California sun. He covered the hole in the wall with a long tapestry until it could be repaired, to prevent the landlord from spotting it.

Neighbors bitched about Terry coming and going at all hours of the night, but the landlord was cool until he strolled into his apartment and inadvertently leaned against the newly hung tapestry, nearly falling through the wall. Once he discovered the hole in his wall and the grease and oil on the carpet, "That did it," Terry said. "I had to move out." Before Terry packed his shit and departed, a brother repaired and framed the hole, a Vago installed new drywall over the damaged wall, another brother mudded and textured the area, another brother painted the wall, and still another member of the green cult replaced the living room and bedroom carpeting.

"You could never tell there was a hole in the wall or that I had built a chopper in the bedroom," Terry noted.

This was a challenging period for motorcycle clubs. During the 1970s, motorcycle clubs were under the scrutiny of law-enforcement agencies looking into gang and drug activity. Bikers and clubs began to organize as a means of survival. Vago chapters took on orderly, weekly meetings. Most of the chapters were represented at monthly officer meetings that dealt with heavy business, and annual national elections took place. Parts took on a Vago leadership role as president of his San Gabriel chapter, and he ultimately became international president (IP).

> With the help of a brother, he tore a hole in the stucco and stud wall leading into the living room with sledgehammers and pry bars.

"He thought through an issue before he acted," Terry said of Parts.

"Time is always on our side," Parts said of being a leader. "When it's the proper time, we'll act."

It was a time of wild, chromed-out, unreliable choppers, built by men with little mechanical experience but packed with passion for the open road.

"We couldn't ride in a pack for 12 miles without a breakdown," Terry said, but his fellow riders had a growing desire to cut a dusty trail for parts unknown.

Just after his long, chopped Panhead fired for the first time, he rode across town to One-Eyed Willie's pad. Willie was a senior member and Terry was the youngster of the bunch.

"He admired my bike, and then tried to take it away," Terry said. "I wasn't having any of that. I only saw him on a bike once. He thought he was tough, but he wasn't much of a rider." Willie was a short, wiry, little-bitty guy; charismatic, but evil.

"He would turn from a smiling nice guy to violent bastard in a hot flash," Terry said.

Willie was in and out of prison constantly, and there was always an evil challenge behind his direct gaze. He liked trikes and constantly worked on severe modifications to turn a 45-cubic-inch, Servi-car trike into a 74-cubic-inch, three-wheeled Shovelhead that was capable of keeping up with any pack of outlaws. He smoked cigarettes, and as the tough years passed his dirty long blond hair turned gray, as did his full beard. He finally finished a trike but flipped it, resulting in a broken hip and a cast that seemed to be a fixture on Willie's hip for years. Willie's luck seemed to only get worse; eventually the Monterey chapter member died of cancer at sixty-two years of age.

Terry rode the Panhead as he learned the Vago ways, ways that involved relentless warfare with other clubs. In the summer of 1972, the height of the reds, whiskey, and weed era, inter-club warfare escalated to a new level. In the desert town of Indio, two Vagos, Hard Times and Spider, were shot off a

He would turn from a smiling nice guy to violent bastard in a hot flash.

Corvair trike. They were stragglers roaming into a sleepy town turned violent behind drugs and rampant club expansion. All the clubs were fighting and jumping members of other clubs, especially inadvertent stragglers.

According to police Lt. Wayne Hoy, the fatal shootings occurred at 3:00 p.m. in the northbound lane of California 86, just inside Coachella. The bikers were shot with a handgun from a passing vehicle. Hard Times was a San Gabriel Valley member rolling through town by himself with only Spider, a young Berdoo member, packing. They both died that hot desert day, and no one was arrested for the shootings.

Tension continued to escalate. Vago Butch was stabbed near the El California café, and his old lady was run over by a car.

Butch was the president of the San Gabriel chapter and a mentor when Terry joined the Vagos. Butch and his longtime girlfriend, a cute blonde babe, stumbled into a violent scene in the parking lot of the café. Someone attacked Joint, a skinny, stringy-haired member of the Vagos Monterey chapter, and stabbed him in the neck. Butch, who wasn't much of a fighter but had heart, attacked the assailants, members of a rival club. Butch was also stabbed in the stomach, but the blonde came to his rescue. She wasn't really a biker babe and didn't know about the code for motorcycle mamas. Her old man was being attacked and she jumped into the center of the fray. One of the escaping bikers ran over her foot with his car. Fortunately, the couple both survived to be life-long partners.

Vago Butch was stabbed near the El California cafe, and his old lady was run over by a car.

"Joint never spoke too well after that," Terry said of his neck wound.

The smoldering town erupted in violence and it spread to the Coachella Valley. A young member of the Warlords MC was attacked in a Denny's restaurant and beaten badly. When he staggered into the street, the rival club members torched his motorcycle.

Ultimately, the National Guard was called in to quell the biker wars. They surrounded the local hospital in the sweltering heat to prevent bikers from entering the hospital and taking revenge on a biker who was in the hospital at the time. He would soon be joined by others. Four more bikers were hospitalized from gunshot and stab wounds after a fight inside Jaime's bar, just outside Coachella on the highway. Two more members were treated at the hospital after a fight with chains.

Coachella Police Chief Lester O'Neil said the gang members came, "from all over the state," and that they had come to the Coachella-Indio area Saturday because of the annual motorcycle rally sponsored by the American Motorcycle Association. The prudish AMA event, located in a quiet, isolated desert community, was the perfect location for this battle for prominence. Each club wanted to make a stand-up name for itself.

> "We beat up anyone and everyone we encountered," Terry said. "It didn't matter what club or affiliation."

The blistering summer sun baking the streets and the drug-soaked brain cells of the bikers set the perfect Western scene for a fight.

"We beat up anyone and everyone we encountered," Terry said. "It didn't matter what club or affiliation."

"We have some 5,000 non-outlaw members of the motorcycle association here," O'Neil said, "and they haven't caused us any trouble. The trouble came from the so-called 'outlaw' gangs who have decided to hold a rally of their own."

Poodle, the rider who started the Vagos, and several other members quit because of the pervasive violence.

After the summer heat, Terry's Panhead started to rattle, and he rode it to Part's' house. "Check it out, will ya," Terry said.

"Rev it up," Parts said to Terry, who sat on the idling chopper. He was prepared to adjust the antiquated bronze Linkert carburetor.

Terry snapped the throttle. The rear exhaust valve stuck and the piston slammed against the hardened steel valve and shattered the cast cylinder. That was the end of the original Pan engine. Depressed, Terry caught a ride home and walked to Ritchie's Café to drown his sorrows in a hot cup of Joe. He sat next to Harry Baker, a loner friend who never joined a club, and spilled his guts.

"Whatcha gonna do?" Harry asked him.

"I need to catch some extra jobs and raise $600 for a new top end," Terry answered. During that era, a common way to obtain more performance and more reliability from a Pan was to adopt a Shovelhead top end: heads, cylinders, intake manifold, and carburetor.

Harry yanked out the long leather wallet chained to his side and peeled off six $100 bills.

"Get it done," Harry said and finished his coffee.

And that's how Terry's Panhead, named *Lady and the Tramp*, received its first transformation.

Throughout this period Terry continued to work for various studios with Harry Woolman. Harry's daughter Pam began an acting career of her own, beginning in 1966 when she appeared as the Tahitian dancer in the film, *On Her Bed of Roses*, with Ronald Warren, Sandra Lynn, and Barbara Hines. The film was later

Riverside cops confiscated a number of Terry's bikes, including *Lady and the Tramp* during 1996 raid. As usual, all his possessions were returned.

Terry snapped the throttle. The rear exhaust valve stuck and the piston slammed against the hardened steel valve and shattered the cast cylinder. That was the end of the original Pan engine.

renamed *Psychedelic Sexualis*. She also played a real dish in the 1965 television series, *Mr. Roberts*. By the 1970s, she had a five-year contract with Warner Brothers, but her personal life was headed toward upheaval, with one bad relationship after another. While Terry was off pursuing the life of a one-percenter, Pam remained on a piece of rural family property in Acton, where she raised sheep, goats, a couple of cows, and horses.

"She had no services out there," Terry said, "And the VW her dad bought her would break down every other trip. We had to haul water and food out to her cheap clapboard house, but she loved working with animals."

Pam banged from one dreamy relationship to another, but Terry was always on hand to help pick up the pieces.

Before she turned twenty she hooked up with a veterinarian and ran off to the University of California at Davis to study to be a vet. After a couple of years, she returned to Los Angeles and the studios, where she went to work, checking in with central casting on a daily basis. Then she hooked up with Dennis Wilson, who was a heroin addict. Wilson, who died on December 28, 1983, had been a founding member and the drummer of The Beach Boys. Wilson got Pam into heroin, which almost killed her.

Pam met a studio dolly operator, Nick Papalasky, in Hawaii on the studio set for *Quigley Down Under*, starring Tom Selleck. Nick was a party guy who couldn't control his drinking. They married, and her grandparents bought them a home in the City of Industry, California. But when she flew to Hawaii to surprise Nick, she found another girl asleep in his hotel room bed and the relationship collapsed.

More than a couple of times, Terry was called to the scene.

Then she hooked up with
the Beach Boys' drummer,
Dennis Wilson, who was a
heroin addict.

Terry the Tramp and Pam on their wedding day at her Grass Valley Ranch. They grew up
together, but she was spent from excesses of the 1960s and her wandering nature could not
compete with his club dedication.

Pam returned from Hawaii and her dad built her and her sister a pair of three-bedroom custom homes behind their original El Monte homestead property. Donna moved out and Alma rented one of the homes to a recovering 5150 case (Section 5150 of the California Welfare and Institutions Code allows a qualified officer or clinician to involuntarily confine a person deemed to have a mental disorder that makes them a danger to himself or herself, and/or others). The renter turned violent, slapped Pam, and threatened Alma. This was one of the times Terry received an urgent call.

He immediately climbed aboard his Panhead and flew across town. At that juncture of his life no two people on earth were more important to him than Pam and Alma. He rode directly into the backyard, kicked out his sidestand, and met Alma in the driveway.

"It wasn't that bad, Terry," Alma said, but he knew otherwise.

"I pounded on his door," Terry said. "When the tenant opened the door, he thought he was a big bag of chips and more."

As soon as he opened his mouth Terry fired on him. "He wasn't even a pretzel," Terry recalled. The tenant immediately departed and never returned.

After a stint with another woman, a tall, dark-haired hippy, Pam bought a 55-acre ranch in Grass Valley and raised goats and horses. She enjoyed the outdoors, hunting, fishing, hiking, and riding motorcycles. Terry spent the holidays with her and they took horse and buggy rides to Nevada City.

"I told him I would introduce him to the gates of hell," Terry said.

"It was a step back in time," Terry said. Folks rode horses and strolled through town drinking hot cocoa and singing Christmas carols. It was amazing, but a culture shock for the outlaw from Los Angeles.

Pam drifted into another relationship and had twins through artificial insemination, Cody and Cheyenne, but Pam's new husband abused her and once more Terry intervened.

"He was an ex-Marine," Terry said, "and thought he was tough."

As soon as the call came, Terry confronted the six-foot two-inch heavy drinker and his red, bulbous nose.

"I told him I would introduce him to the gates of hell," Terry said. Instead of taking Terry up on his offer, the husband departed. He ended up in a Utah prison for hustling women.

During the summer of 1975, seven members of the Vagos mustered the balls to undertake a run to Texas to visit a long-time member, Chainsaw, in Dennison. There, Chainsaw owned and operated a shop, The Iron Horse. The trip began one night while Terry and his club brothers sat in their sacred Denny's in El Monte. Terry turned to another young member, J.J., whom he had given his full patch just a year earlier.

"I've got a new top end on my bike," Terry said. "Let's ride to Texas."

"I've got to go to work," J.J. replied.

J.J. was a tree trimmer for the city of Baldwin Park. But his true priorities were chasing girls and playing poker, both of which took precedence over riding his chopped Knucklehead. He was a short, good-looking brother with long, sandy blonde hair, a long, carefully trimmed mustache, and brilliant white even teeth that he bared often.

Terry looked at his stepbrother, Parts, and then back at J.J. It was every outlaw's dream to ride across the county, but the nasty reputation that followed most riders wearing club patches made such excursions treacherous. Every scared citizen in every seedy small town represented potential trouble. From pushy straights to overzealous police to territorial clubs, the potential for danger ran high. In most small burghs, bikers were allowed only the courtesy of a gas stop before being escorted to the city limits.

Every scared citizen in every seedy small town represented potential trouble.

The brothers tossed the notion around and voted to head out. Things went well enough until they got to Amarillo, Texas, where another biker, a member of the Bandidos MC, scrutinized the scruffy Vagos at a gas station.

He followed Terry around, trying to get a look at the patch on his back while checking out Terry's bike. Tired of his staring, Terry confronted the man.

"Whatta ya need?" Terry asked gruffly.

The Bandido responded with another question: "What club are you with?"

"Vagos," Terry replied. "What of it?"

"I'm with the Bandidos," he said, flatly. "We run this area."

"Well then," Terry said, "you must know where we can get a good steak and be left alone, right?"

"I think I can help you out," the Bandido returned. "Ride up to the Harley dealer; I'll meet you there."

Terry and his brothers rode to the dealer, but when the Bandido didn't show, they rode down the street to a Denny's, which became Terry's unofficial office wherever he went. As they settled into a long, upholstered booth, Terry noted a pack of fifteen Bandidos pulling into the dealership.

Parts rode back to Amarillo Harley-Davidson and told the Bandidos about their mission to party with the Banshees and visit their brother. The Banshees Motorcycle Club USA was founded in New Orleans, Louisiana in the spring of 1966. Chainsaw, a retired Vago, returned to his hometown of Dennison, Texas, an oil-rich town, to be near his family. Denison is located in northeastern Grayson County on U.S. Highway 75. It's only seventy-five miles north of Dallas and four miles south of the Texas/Oklahoma border. State Highway 120 passes through Denison from east to west, and State Highway 84 borders northern Denison.

Chainsaw stayed in touch with Terry and Parts after he opened his shop. He met local members of the Banshees, who didn't hold his Vago membership against him. "We remained friends with the Banshees ever since," Terry said. "When we were in their territories, they took us everywhere. They helped repair our motorcycles, partied with us, stood beside us in bar brawls, and treated us like family."

The group spent two weeks in Amarillo with the Banshees, then rode on to Dennison, which borders gently rolling and wooded terrain stretching northward to the shores of Lake Texoma and the Red River. They met up with the Scorpions MC at Dennison and partied another two weeks. The Scorpions Motorcycle club was established in Detroit in 1966 in the basement of a young member's home. His mom, Pearl, made the members check their guns at the door. She carefully placed their weapons in a wooden cabinet and they could pick them up when they left the underground clubhouse. Their next clubhouse was blown up by a rival club.

In 1976 members of the Scorpions played starring roles in the international cult classic motorcycle film, *Northville Cemetery Massacre*, in which a young girl is raped and her father and the police wage a bloody battle against the members of a motorcycle gang that recently arrived in town. The violent action saga starred David Hyry and Carson Jackson, but Nick Nolte overdubbed the voice of one of the characters. In a typical Hollywood plot twist for that era of anti-heroes, the bikers were innocent and the vigilante mob had targeted the wrong culprits. Not that it helped in real life; like every other motorcycle club during that era, the Scorpions were the target of constant harassment from law enforcement officials. This despite the club having a reputation as being comprised of solid, law-abiding citizens, striving to live up to the Scorpions motto: "Family plus job plus club equals brotherhood."

The Scorpions might not have been the type of outlaws who actually broke laws, but they still knew how to have a good time. The Scorpion philosophy might have put them on the right side of the law, but it also included hard riding, having a good time, and

> His mom, Pearl, made the members check their guns at the door. She carefully placed their weapons in a wooden cabinet and they could pick them up when they left the underground clubhouse.

causing havoc. This type of club, which Sonny Barger of the Hells Angels calls a "mom-and-pop" club, holds a lot of appeal for many motorcyclists, offering the support and camaraderie of a family without the criminal baggage often associated with outlaw clubs. The Scorpions thrived, spreading into a number of other states. As the club grew they established chapters in Danville, Virginia; Lee County, North Carolina; Dallas, South Dallas, and Wichita Falls, Texas; and Oakland County, Monroe, and Coldwater, Michigan.

"They invited us to a party out on a farm," Terry remembered. "They had three or four bands, girls, campsites set up all over the area, and a huge farmhouse to party in. We were there four days. Then one of the Banshees, Big Joe Fletcher, asked if we'd like to go for a putt. I said okay, but asked how far we were going. He said it was just down the road."

A hundred miles later, the bikers rode up to one of Joe's favorite stops. After four hours of drinking and playing pool, the group fired up their bikes for the return run. They were in the middle of the open Texas plains, but Joe seemed to know every pit stop between the party and his hangout. When it began to rain and then hail, the riders leaned their choppers into a truck stop to escape the downpour and dry off.

Inside, the welcome was less than friendly. Truckers started muttering obscenities. Amidst the cold stares, one trucker with ham hock-sized forearms grumbled over a beer, wondering aloud, "Who let these grubby motherfuckers in here?'"

Although the club members out-numbered the truckers two to one, the two starkly different philosophies faced off over checkered linoleum and vinyl swivel stools around a half-moon café counter. The hardworking middle-class citizen confronted the non-working, middle-class renegade. The men in the greasy ball caps and tightly cropped hair didn't understand the men with the long manes, greasy Levi's, and a taste for adventure.

"You longhaired faggots must be from California, and I suggest that you just keep movin' your asses in that direction!"

The big-fisted trucker slammed a clenched side of beef on the counter and stood up.

"You longhaired faggots must be from California, and I suggest that you just keep movin' your asses in that direction!"

Several truckers pushed back their chairs and stood up. Two more rounded the counter corner clutching pool cues. The threats and ridicule continued until Terry stepped forward and stood face-to-face with the barrel-chested trucker.

"We've been riding for a while" he said, bluntly. "We're tired, hungry, and it's hailing beer cans outside. You can either back off and let us be or we're going to go to blows."

His eyes bore into the bigger man, and violence hung in the air like a dark February fog as Terry broke the silence engulfing the room. "And you'll be the first to fall."

The big trucker wasn't intimidated. He threw the first punch, triggering an all-out brawl as pool cues whipped through the air, chairs and tables tumbled, and fists flew. Terry and the big man stood toe-to-toe and exchanged blows.

Pushed against the counter, his nose broken and bleeding, having felt the intensity of Terry's unrelenting fists and his adrenaline-powered fury, the trucker now understood that the bikers meant business. When the man raised his hands to indicate submission, Terry respected the surrender and called for the other bikers to stop fighting.

A handful of the truckers escaped or were thrown out into the hail to find their way to their trucks, but the bikers stayed long enough for the weather to let up and to underscore their triumphant point. This run to Texas opened the door for Vagos members to experience the open road in search of women, action, and adventure.

The Vagos left the Banshees behind in Denison and headed west, but they weren't alone. In Gainesville, they rolled through town and spotted a steakhouse. "We rolled into the parking lot, parked

This run to Texas opened the door for Vagos members to experience the open road in search of women, action, and adventure.

and checked our bikes," Terry said. "We strolled into the restaurant, and it was as if we owned the place. They treated us good, and someone picked up the tab."

They started their raucous, sparkling chrome choppers, popped wheelies, and peeled down the street to a bar.

"You couldn't just walk into a bar; you had to knock on the door," Terry said. As they approached the door a tall good-looking cowboy wearing polished Justin cowboy boots and a tall western hat walked up to Wolfman and Terry.

"Suddenly every patron in the bar pulled a handgun," Terry said, **"and we were looking down the barrel of his shotgun."**

"Good evening girls," he said and knocked on the door.

"It was on," Terry said, "and we went to blows." The fight only lasted a minute before the door opened and the cowboy was pulled inside.

The Vagos followed him in, took a table, and a waitress approached to take their orders. The western bar ran the long length of the building on the left. Two dark pool tables resided at the back of the room and heavy, polished wooden tables were set in the center. The seven Vagos pulled up chairs and sat down. In less than a couple of minutes, the bubbly waitress returned with a tray full of drinks. She set the saloon-printed napkins on the table after carefully wiping it down. Then she set the drinks down, smiled, and stepped away without asking for payment. Mellow country and western music drifted from a glistening jukebox.

Joking and kidding about the fight at the door, the members reached for their whiskey- and tequila-filled tumblers when the door opened and in walked a half-dozen tall, stout cowboys, the biggest cowboys Terry had ever laid eyes on. Leading the group was a slick gentleman carrying a chromed, sawed-off shotgun across his chest.

"He looked like Boss Hogg from the *Dukes of Hazard*," Terry said.

"I picked up your dinner, boys," Boss Hogg said in a dead serious Texas drawl. "You've had something to drink, and now it's time you got on your bicycles and left Texas."

Parts was always ready for a fight and mouthed off something about finishing his drink.

"Suddenly every patron in the bar pulled a handgun," Terry said, "and we were looking down the barrel of his shotgun."

"The choice is simple," said the big man the others referred to as Falcon. "You can leave Texas or go directly to McAlester Prison," referring to the infamous Oklahoma State Penitentiary that housed many convicts from Texas.

"We set our drinks back down and peeled out," Terry said. ☠

Terry and the Sundowner

THE SUMMER HEAT OF 1975 baked the Mojave Desert between Vegas and Barstow, California with 110 degrees of unpleasantness as a twenty-five-year-old clubber, his little redheaded secretary wrapped tightly around him, rumbled toward Los Angeles and the *Easyriders* magazine offices.

"I was delivering the saga of sagas to share with the motorcycling world," Puppy said. He was determined to meet the magazine's editor and pitch his epic. Little did the lanky biker know he was about to change directions. Between the seizure-inducing light show of Las Vegas and bleak desert nothingness of Barstow there's a strange road to nowhere called Zzyzx. There's no town, only miles and miles of Joshua trees, creosote brush, and road debris bordering the asphalt ribbon.

Puppy rode a vintage 1937 Harley-Davidson flathead 80. It was black and ugly, with a 7-inch over-extended H-D springer. It was cool-looking until he traveled; then he bolted on the full-valence front fender and added stock leather saddlebags for

> Between the seizure-inducing light show of Las Vegas and bleak desert nothingness of Barstow there's a strange road to nowhere called Zzyzx.

packing. He bought this bike in 1964, so it already carried a decade of his outlaw history as a member of the Sundowners, another national club with chapters in ten states and the mother chapter in Ogden, Utah.

The bike reverberated with the sound of solid lifters and upswept fishtail pipes that slapped their harsh note against the surrounding mountainside bordering the Mojave National Preserve. Puppy and his girl rumbled along at 80 miles per hour heading directly for the Devil's Playground, a large, sandy region of the Mojave Desert stretching more than 40 miles into the preserve.

Puppy was flying, his long red hair slapping against the frumpy crimson-haired secretary holding tight to his vibrating torso. Puppy always rode like a man possessed. One time while traveling from Florida to New York to visit his mom, several Hells Angels chased him for three days. He grew up with these guys and they knew how to ride, but not well enough to keep up with Puppy.

"They couldn't catch me," Puppy said, "so they went to my mom's house on the third day and had coffee with her while they waited for me to show up."

Puppy and his secretary rumbled up the incline toward the Zzyzx Junction, his typewriter strapped on the back of his tall sissy bar and 132 epic chapters of loose-leaf manuscript bundled in the saddlebags, when his rear Goodyear Eagle tire hissed and deflated.

The old motorcycle spit from side to side and Puppy fought for control as he veered onto the gravel-strewn emergency lane. He was pissed and boiling in the simmering heat. His secretary tentatively dismounted and they studied the damaged rear tire. There was nothing for him to do but remove his classic biker leather jacket and black leather cut, drape them across the solo seat, and start pushing the apehanger handlebars on the 500-pound motorcycle laden with luggage and his manuscript.

The deflated tire caused the bike to blubber back and forth and added substantial drag. A late-model Ford Grand Torino slid into the emergency lane and skidded to a stop.

"Can I help?" hollered Terry the Tramp from the driver's seat.

"Yeah," Puppy barked back. "Get that fucking thing outta my way."

"No," Terry said, "can I give you a hand?"

Sweat ran down Puppy's face, but he kept pushing, and shoved the flathead into the truck lane and alongside the Torino. "Unless ya got a pocket full of air, you can't help."

Just then, a slick BMW rider wearing a full leather suit and full-face helmet pulled off the highway in front of the Torino. He dismounted, sized up the situation, and approached Puppy.

"I just bought a can of this new Fix-a-Flat in Vegas," he said. "If you can cover the $4, it's yours."

Puppy gave him the cash and Terry and Puppy crawled around the hot motorcycle in the desert heat, positioning the valve stem for a refill.

"I'm Terry," Terry said. "I'm a Vago."

Puppy was well aware of a recent conflict between the Vagos and the Sundowners, but he was too pissed-off about his flat tire predicament to consider the political ramifications.

"I'm Puppy," he said. "I'm a Sundowner."

Terry didn't hesitate to extend his hand. "I'll take your girl in the car," Terry said, "while you test this shit out."

The tire aired up and seemed to hold. Puppy kicked his bike to life and pulled onto the freeway. As he rolled through the gears and gained speed and confidence, the heat from the smoldering asphalt and pavement friction exacerbated the weakness in the tire structure. It blew out and sent Puppy sideways and off the side of the highway once more.

Terry again rambled off the freeway in front of Puppy and backed within range. He immediately jumped out of the slick air-conditioned sedan and popped open the massive trunk. He grabbed some tools and in short order removed the trunk lid and tossed it into the desert, where it rested among years of highway debris, hubcaps, and whiskey bottles.

"Let's load it in the trunk," Terry said.

"Are you kidding?" Puppy asked, stepping into the desert to retrieve the trunk lid.

"We can do it," Terry said.

"But this car is almost new," Puppy said.

"It's just a car," Terry said. "I'll get another one."

They hoisted the Lady 80 into the trunk and shoved the trunk lid in between the motorcycle and the back of the massive sedan, then lashed it down. Terry pulled out into the traveling lanes but quickly determined that the additional weight of the heavy motorcycle and his two new passengers caused the wide car tires to rub against the Torino's rear fenders . He pulled off the freeway again, jumped out of the car, found the tire iron in the trunk, and proceeded to wedge the cast iron bar between the fenders and the tires. He pried the steel sheet metal away from the tires until there was ample clearance.

"You're destroying your car," Puppy said.

"It's just a cage," Terry said. "Let's hit it."

They drove directly to Terry's home in El Monte, more than 200 miles into Los Angeles.

"He just had a new baby and his wife and his stepdad were there," Puppy said of the generous biker opening his home to a complete stranger.

Together they removed the flathead 80 from the trunk, replaced the scratched and dented lid, and started to work on the wounded motorcycle. At the time, Terry had a carport next to his house with a small closet attached. He opened the closet and dug out a fully chromed, 16-inch wheel with a virtually new Goodyear Eagle tire mounted.

"I don't have any money," Puppy said.

"That's alright," Terry said. "Either return this wheel or pay me when you have it."

That evening, Terry fed Puppy and his redheaded secretary and put them up. The next morning the group rode to Terry's Denny's restaurant headquarters. That's where Puppy discovered that his host was the president of the San Gabriel Chapter of the Vagos. From time to time, as the coffee shop filled up with members of the green tribe, Puppy tripped on the fact that there had been a recent problem between their clubs. But he never suspected foul play, or a trick back looming as a member made a phone call or two brothers walked outside to discuss something in private.

"I felt like I had met a brother, not a member of another club," Puppy said.

"Puppy thinks he's a Sundowner," Terry said. "But he's really a Vago."

Puppy knew his welcome wasn't everlasting and needed to find his own Sundowner brothers in the Long Beach region. He yanked his leather address book out of his cut and started making calls from the Denny's phone booth. Connection after connection went dead. His list of numbers was outdated.

"Let me see if I can help," Terry said and produced his directory of club members throughout Los Angeles.

"All the numbers worked," Puppy said, slightly embarrassed because Terry was more connected to the region's Sundowners than Puppy was, but he appreciated the help.

Puppy lived in Los Angeles from time to time, since he escaped his home in New Orleans when he was thirteen.

"I had to head west," Puppy said. "You know the drill, 'Go West young man, go West.' " He toiled on rodeo grounds in Texas. He worked for his uncle in Tucson, and worked on a horse ranch while hitchhiking across the country.

> "Puppy thinks he's a Sundowner," Terry said. "But he's really a Vago."

"My hero was Stony Burke. I even dressed like him in those days."

Settling down in Los Angeles this time wasn't a problem and he immediately grabbed a position as a motorcycle mechanic in Santa Monica, but the connection with his club brothers led Puppy down a dark road.

"I contacted Tang, the president of the Long Beach chapter," Puppy said, "but he told me most of the brothers lived in Riverside and they couldn't hook up with me that night. He had numerous restrictions."

Puppy rode to Long Beach, the seaside community just south of the Los Angeles Harbor. He discovered a biker bar called the Why Not on Cherry just south of Signal Hill, the home of a thousand oil wells jutting out of the landscape like the prickly spines on the back of a porcupine. He rolled into the Why Not, finding a dingy bar with a couple of scratched and abused barroom pool tables and a handful of rickety dining tables. It was packed on a Friday summer night and patches were prevalent.

There were Hessians, Mongols, and lots of loners or independent riders, and everyone got along.

"Everyone accepted me," Puppy said. He called Tang, since he lived only a block away.

"We don't go there," Tang said. "We party in Riverside at the Quaff."

Puppy finally hooked up with Tang and Hooch— Larry Harris— a Utah charter member and one of the club's founding members.

"Let's play poker," Tang suggested, inviting Puppy to his home.

"I don't gamble much," Puppy said, "but I'll give it a shot."

Unfortunately he took the pot and it raised Tang's ire. Tang was average build and height, with long, blonde hair and lots of chips on his shoulders.

As the weeks rolled on, Puppy met Smokey and Gimpy at the Quaff Barrel Inn in Riverside, but he found himself staying with Terry and the Vagos. Each time he suggested that the Long Beach Sundowners party with the Vagos, he was turned down by the irascible Tang.

> More than once, Terry and Puppy were back-to-back, taking on anything that came their way.

"When in Rome," Tang said. "We don't party with them."

Finally, on a warm fall evening, Puppy left work and rode to Terry's house in El Monte.

"I'll ride home with you," Terry said, all suited up and ready for the road.

"I couldn't turn them down this time," Puppy said, and Terry, Dago, and Jerry the Jew rode with Puppy to Long Beach, where they met with several Sundowners. The cocky Tang was visibly upset. They rode to a bar in downtown Long Beach and Tang immediately started a fight.

More than once, Terry and Puppy were back-to-back, taking on anything that came their way. "We barely got clear of that place and Tang started another problem at the next bar."

At the third bar, the owner met them at the door and refused entry. The five riders peeled down the street. Tang needed to prove something, and the more he drank, the more the too-tough condition was exacerbated.

As they approached a light on Atlantic Boulevard, the light turned amber and three of the brothers nailed it and peeled through the light. Tang and Dago were stuck and slid to a stop. Dago was a helluva Vago, but he was on parole and couldn't face another problem with the law. While Dago sat on his bike minding his own business, Tang kicked out his kickstand, jumped off his bike, unzipped his fly, and began to urinate in the center of the street. Then he dropped his ignition key and was crawling around the street when the cops arrived.

Dago, in the spirit of brotherhood, stayed with Tang, but as soon as the cops ran his license, his parole situation surfaced. Plus he had no papers for his motorcycle; he was arrested and his motorcycle was impounded.

"He never saw that motorcycle again," Terry said. "It was a shame."

Puppy learned the true meaning of brotherhood from Terry. He moved out of Los Angeles and set up a chapter of the Sundowners in Florida, but he remained on the road most of the time, where he felt most comfortable reaching out to meet his brothers.

"I wanted to know all my brothers when they rolled to our national annual run," Puppy said.

So every year he rode out of Florida, heading north to visit South Carolina chapters, then New York, where he visited his mom and sister. Next, he would peel west to Wisconsin, then Minnesota, and spent long months in Colorado with various chapters, until he rolled into Utah to the mother chapter, then Nevada, Idaho, and finally back to California. Before the summer months were gone, he rode to the national run early so he was set up and ready to greet his arriving brothers. One year, he covered more than 275,000 miles.

Every time he crossed the state line into California, he looked up Terry the Tramp and the Vagos. They would be friends forever. 🕱

Trickbags and Executions

AS THE RECENTLY FORMED VAGO outlaw organization rolled toward the center of the decade, other motorcycle clubs were heading down a profoundly immoral, harmful, and destructive path. It was all about how evil and how tough a charter could be. Brothers were challenged to commit more malevolent acts to prove themselves. Mindless acts of violence were presented as the standard of behavior, as if there was no recourse. Terry witnessed this growing level of wickedness, rising inexorably like the mercury in a thermometer tossed on a bonfire. He considered leaving the club, but then on one hot summer day his Vago fate was sealed.

It was a time of the most deadly drug to fuel the outlaw spirit: reds. The chemical secobarbital sodium, originally developed by Eli Lilly and Company and marketed under the brand name Seconal, was a barbiturate derivative drug first synthesized in 1928. It was sold as a sedative and became a very popular one at that. Seobarbital

A photo of Greg "Silver" White at the age of twenty, in 1974. *Photo copyright © 2011 Silver*

Mindless acts of violence were presented as the standard of behavior, as if there was no recourse.

sodium was found in the lifeless bodies of Judy Garland, Jimi Hendrix, Brian Epstein, Tennessee Williams, and Alan Wilson (singer for the band Canned Heat). It is a primary ingredient in the drug Somulose, which is used to euthanize horses and cattle. In other words, it's some powerful shit.

Popular among celebrity drug addicts for decades, Seconal began to be widely misused by the general public in the 1960s and 1970s, although it became less common with the advent of benzodiazepines. Seconal acquired many nicknames, the most common being "reds," "red devils," or "red dillies" (it was originally packaged in red capsules). Other nicknames included "seccies" and "red hearts." A less common handle was "dolls," and this bit of slang provided the title for Jacqueline Susann's novel, *Valley of the Dolls*, in which the main characters use secobarbital and similar drugs.

Seconal proved popular among motorcycle club members, though some clubs banned its use because it made night riders impervious to fear, turning them into overzealous, indestructible fighters, at least in their own minds. It was notorious for causing fights and enabling brothers to ride like possessed madmen. It also fueled a trick bag that altered Terry's viewpoint about club life.

The term "trick bag" refers to a situation in which a club member is edging another member, or a prospect, into acting out of character or worse, like a woman enticing a man to be unfaithful just because she can. In the mid-1970s, at a party behind a small home in the San Gabriel Valley, a young member, Silver, was thrust into a deadly trap. Two older members, mature men who should have been brotherly leaders, slipped Silver into a trick bag."

Gregory "Silver" White was just a young kid, standing all of five-feet six-inches tall, having the time of his life. In the Vagos he found a brotherhood and a family that liked to ride and party as much as he did. When older brothers offered him a drink, drugs, or a girl, he didn't hesitate. They were his brothers, his extended family, or so

Run to see Silver in 1977 at the Tracy Prison in California. Silver wasn't released until 2010. Vago members helped organize and promote a prison bike show.

he thought. He prospected for the Vagos for a year, never working, just selling reds and acid and being there for his brothers.

"I was a Vago 24/7," Silver said. He had been a member for four months and was still riding and playing hard when two Vago prospects from Pomona ran into members of the Warlords MC at an Ontario party. Both prospects were stabbed and shot, then sent unceremoniously down the road. That set off the president of the Pomona chapter, Pomona Don, a.k.a. Donny Kelso.

In this case, the two brothers enticed their young and inexperienced brother Silver into a murder scheme. Silver had been partying all weekend and was still loaded on reds, so he was utterly convinced he could do anything.

"He didn't even know where he was," Terry said. "On reds it was all fun and wild pranks."

Pomona Don devised a scheme to get revenge on the Warlords. They discovered their target inside an industrial park

Silver had been partying all weekend and was still loaded on reds, so he was utterly convinced he could do anything.

Donny Kelso, the ringleader, in the late 1970s at the gates to San Quentin. He was transferred to a working ranch during the last years of his sentence. *Photo copyright © 2011 Silver*

fabrication shop, Custom Design and Fabrication, in the City of Industry. It was 4:30 in the afternoon when David Dupras, nineteen, of Torrance, Charles Evans, thirty-four, of Lawndale, Donald "Donny" Kelso, twenty-five, of Ontario, and Gregory "Silver" White, twenty, of Rowland Heights, invaded the industrial park unit. One of the four fired a single shot into the back of the head of Adlebert Milo Hempy, twenty-six, of Ontario.

Things didn't go as planned. For starters, their first victim wasn't a member of the Warlocks. Hempy didn't belong to any club; he was a loner employee, just doing his job. The attack started out badly and went south from there. Pantaleon Sanchez, twenty-nine, the shop owner and president of the Warlords chapter—their intended target—arrived at the shop after running errands and interrupted the melee. Another carload of Vagos arrived and one of the members shot Sanchez once in the leg through the door of his pickup, but Sanchez was able to speed away and alert the Los Angeles Sheriff's Department.

Silver astride Parts's chopper in 1977, at the rare Tracy Prison bike show. During this era, prisoners were able to don their patches and once more be a part of the Vago brotherhood for an afternoon. *Photo copyright © 2011 Silver*

"Everything went to hell once we were inside the shop," Silver said. "The intention wasn't to kill anyone until we stepped into the interior and one member decided he was going to show them how tough Vagos could be."

The Vagos faced certain doom. The car full of members sped away, but two workers were still sequestered in the shop with the angry, drugged, gun-wielding members. They attempted to force both employees into their 1967 Impala, but one broke free and escaped—another potential witness on the loose. They succeeded in forcing young Michael O'Hara, twenty-six, of Pomona, who was a mechanic in the shop and a Warlords member, at gunpoint into the two-door vehicle with the four Vagos. They drove him thirteen miles to a rural area between Chino and Ontario.

Calls to local law enforcement describing the Impala had already been made by the time the four Vagos drove off the Pomona Freeway at the Long View exit. They skidded under the freeway and around a dusty corner. O'Hara was forced to lie down in the dirt at the side of the road, where Donny shot him three times in the head.

Loaded on reds, they had the fire-breathing balls to drive back toward the City of Industry. They spun around, drove under the

"Everything went to hell once we were inside the shop," Silver said. "The intention wasn't to kill anyone until we stepped into the interior and one member decided he was going to show them how tough Vagos could be."

freeway toward the on-ramp and got as far as the Pomona Freeway ramp when two undercover sheriff's deputies recognized their vehicle. The plainclothes sedan rolled off the freeway as they sped up the on-ramp. The officers spun around and gave chase. The cops pulled them over and arrested the four suspects handily. Still stoned out of their minds, they offered no resistance and were booked on suspicion of murder and kidnapping. All the guns were discovered in the car, according to San Bernardino County authorities.

This heinous incident took less than one hour on a sunny Southern California day, yet it haunted families, whole clubs, and individuals for a lifetime. One of the instigators was Charles Evans, who went by the nickname Mute Tommy. He turned on the others and received only three and a half years in jail. He had long, stringy, red hair and a curly red beard, and the rat was grubby to the bone, but he was the first to see through the effects of the reds. Given the devastating position in which he found himself immersed, he began to talk, using sign language.

"He was a deaf mute," Silver said. "They brought in an interpreter. Tommy spilled his guts, even though he had stayed in the car and didn't come in the shop."

After they were arrested they were transported directly to the City of Industry Sheriff's station and jailed separately. Silver was immediately arraigned on two counts of first-degree murder, charged with being the gunman at two shootings and denied bail due to special circumstances. The others were afforded $100,000 bail, but none could raise the funds to be released. Silver immediately asked to make a phone call and lawyered up. That was enough to stop any interrogation, but because he had no money, he was supplied with a public defender.

A group shot taken at the prison bike show in 1977. When this photo was taken in 1977, prisons had yet to be switched to punishment yards. Many programs like the bike show were denied in future years. *Photo copyright © 2011 Silver*

The PD separated his trial from the others and moved it from Pomona to downtown Los Angeles. They asked for a judge-only trial, with a black judge who openly fought the death sentence. Within two weeks Silver was convicted of two counts of first-degree murder, kidnapping, assault to commit murder, and four gun allegations.

The trials for the other three took place between his conviction and sentencing. Donny Kelso, at five feet, six inches, with scraggly brown hair and full beard—the shortest, most senior member—was the mastermind behind the act of revenge. In a matter of hours the Pomona Chapter member's act of overt toughness had blown up in his face. He came down from his chest-pounding high and realized he was behind bars, and would be for years to come.

Thief, or David Dupras, was another young Los Angeles member. He had no concept of his drug-induced actions. He was just a nineteen-year-old kid who thought he was stepping up with his brothers to "take care of business." He had no notion of the gravity of the situation until the drugs and whiskey wore off. Tall, at over six feet,

This shot captured Kelso in the San Quentin State Prison visiting room with one of his daughters. *Photo copyright © 2011 Silver*

with long, dark black hair, Thief was under the age required to be approved as a full member of the Vagos. The limit was twenty-one.

"He had to have a connection to slip in under the age limit," Silver said, "So did I. I was one month from turning twenty-one when this went down."

"I'll stay in this club until we can get Silver out," Terry said. With that, Terry sealed his fate as a Vago and kept his promise, but the mindless violence that had landed his brothers in prison made a permanent impression on the man. He remained tough and vigilant, but did everything in his power to keep brothers away from stupid, life-devastating decisions.

> **Within two weeks he was convicted of two counts of first-degree murder, kidnapping, assault to commit murder, and four gun allegations.**

"Terry and his brother Parts took me under their wing," Silver said.

After the second-degree conviction of Donny and Thief and the manslaughter conviction of Mute Tommy,

Terry the Tramp visiting Silver in the Oregon State Penitentiary where Silver served the last fourteen years of his sentence. California has an interstate compact and can transfer prisoners anywhere in the country for various reasons. It took Silver three years to be approved for transfer to a facility closer to his parent's home. *Photo copyright © 2011 Silver*

Silver's convictions were altered to one first-degree murder and one second-degree murder in addition to the other convictions of kidnapping, assault, and gun charges. He was given life plus five with a minimum of seven years.

It wasn't until his eleventh year that he was finally allowed a parole hearing, but he was denied parole under Governor Pete Wilson.

"I should have been paroled in June of 1995," Silver said, "but legal perceptions were changing."

He was turned down because the board didn't feel the judgment properly reflected the severity of the crime. "Parole is not supposed to be based on the severity of the crime," Silver said. "That never changes, but if the prisoner no longer poses a threat, or has been properly rehabilitated, he should be considered. Terry and the club hooked me up with an attorney and we fought the finding until 2009."

Because of changing laws Donny and Thief fell into a lucky break and were released in 1982 after just six and one-half years. During his stay in Folsom, Donny lucked into meeting Debbie, a young California girl who started corresponding with prisoners. He married her in 1977. In 1986 he was once again incarcerated after being convicted of home invasion and robbery. While Donny was back in Folsom, Debbie returned to visit often. Donny died in Folsom prison of hepatitis after his liver shut down in 1988, but Debbie continued to visit Silver at the facility and in 1989 the young Vago married the strawberry blonde, who had two sons by Donny. She stuck by him and was at his side when Governor Arnold Schwarzenegger afforded Silver a parole date in 2009 after 35 years. The governor changed the prison system's title from the Department of Corrections to the Department of Corrections and Rehabilitation.

"There weren't many rehab programs for high-security level prisoners," Silver said. "In fact at some facilities the only program available was a drug and alcohol NA meeting. When I asked for more they told me to go to the library and write book reports."

When Silver was granted a paroled transfer from Sacramento to Arizona, his Sacramento brothers gave him Bugsy, a pug. "I missed dogs and motorcycles while I was in prison," Silver said. *Photo copyright © 2011 Silver*

"I always stood by the code that the individual's actions reflect on the whole," Silver said. "All you have in prison is your word."

When Silver was released from prison, the club gave him this 2000 Softail. Spike rebuilt and tuned it in preparation for Silver's release. *Photo copyright © 2011 Silver*

During the time he spent in prison, he remained an active Vago. "I always stood by the code that the individual's actions reflect on the whole," Silver said. "All you have in prison is your word."

During his incarceration he spent time in a number of California correctional facilities, including Chino, Tracy, Vacaville, Folsom, and San Quentin, and he also did time in the Oregon State Prison. Silver was finally released on parole on January 26, 2010. "I'm on a no-contact-with-the-club parole stipulation," Silver said, "but as soon as I'm cut loose I will be an active Vago again."

Albuquerque Hell

SEVERAL EVENTS SHAPED THE FUTURE OF THE VAGOS, setting the stage for Terry's leadership style. Many factors influenced the ways in which the Vagos MC matured during the 1970s. One of them involved the nature of the motorcycles built by Harley-Davidson during the dark years when the company was owned by American Machinery and Foundry (AMF), which had purchased the company in the late 1960s. This precipitated a dramatic decrease in quality control. During this period Harley was shipping bikes to dealerships that were so poorly built they often had to be overhauled before leaving the showroom floor.

At the same time the manufacturers from Japan were beginning to build big bikes of their own, machines like the Honda CB750 and the Kawasaki Z1. The vast majority of riders bought the Japanese machines instead of the shoddy bikes coming from Milwaukee, but that was not an option for most members of one-percenter motorcycle clubs. The clubs had been created in large part by veterans of World War II and the Korean War, and many of them required their members to ride only bikes built by American companies. After the demise of Indian in the 1950s, that meant bikes built by Harley-Davidson, so club members were stuck riding Harleys regardless of how unreliable they had become.

When the Vagos first started out, the mechanical fragility of their chopped Harleys governed how far they dared travel from their home base. They had limited mechanical experience, but they had guts and a passion for freedom. They wanted to ride fast and be left alone to wander the streets in search of adventure. Club members gradually learned more about motorcycle mechanics and ventured farther from their homes in Covina and El Monte.

> The bikers were forced to search within their own charters for mechanically minded brothers when seeking the knowledge, expertise, and parts needed to keep their long, unruly choppers on the road.

Even after they improved their mechanical abilities, other factors limited their freedom to roam. For example, even if they had the mechanical skill to fix a bike that broke down, getting parts could be a problem. For much of the 1960s and 1970s, and even into the 1980s, Harley-Davidson dealers wouldn't have anything to do with marijuana-smoking, beer-swilling, long-haired bikers who sought parts, help, knowledge, or basic service work. Dealers turned them away and refused to work on modified motorcycles. The bikers were forced to search within their own charters for mechanically minded brothers when seeking the knowledge, expertise, and parts needed to keep their long, unruly choppers on the road.

As the 1970s got underway, help came from other sources. A chopper industry was growing like rust on the hull of a sunken ship. Society, cops, and Harley-Davidson wanted the worn-out, corroding hulk to remain on the bottom and deteriorate, but chopper riders wouldn't accept failure. They hated cops, the Man, family life, the government—you name it. They didn't trust anyone, and the Vietnam War and the Watergate era inflamed their inclination to distrust the establishment. They were young men in the search of true brotherhood. A wild, free spirit flourished, like a captured hawk released. They were warriors without a war, searching for a fight and unencumbered sex. They wanted adventure, and the lure of the open road proved irresistible, especially after the 1969 movie *Easy Rider* challenged riders to head across the country.

Most parts for choppers came from the hulks of old Harleys, but aftermarket components were beginning to appear from companies like Paughco. Paughco stamped out tin parts for other industries until the owner's son, Ron Paugh, approached his dad with a hard-to-find Harley component, a bent tin primary cover, and the wheels began to turn. Soon the company was stamping out custom motorcycle parts. Still, chopper riders were a poor lot, always looking for a deal or a salvageable used part.

> They were warriors without a war, searching for a fight and unencumbered sex.

In 1975, five of Terry's brother Vagos took off cross-country in a flashy orange van to score motorcycle parts in club member Ron Keine's hometown of Detroit. In the custom-painted party vehicle, Ron, Doc, Grubby, Ten-Speed, and Sandman flew along Interstate 40, through Albuquerque, New Mexico They planned to cut a dusty trail to Detroit, Michigan, where three of them grew up, but all hell broke loose in the rural open West.

It was the evening of February 8, 1974, when the brothers hit the road. The Vagos had a strict rule. The only excuse for missing a mandatory meeting was jail. They attended the February 8 meeting and peeled out. They had to return by February 15 for the next meeting. All five were in their twenties and they all had previous run-ins with the law, but for minor offenses. Doc Greer, Art Smith, and Ron hailed from Michigan. Tom Gladish and Sandman Smith were Californian natives. Doc and Art Smith were cousins.

Operating on a tight budget, they shared pancakes at a restaurant, because it was the cheapest bulky item on the menu. In some cases they choose beer over food, and Doc paid for gas with a stolen credit card. They flew through Albuquerque without stopping, but

Ron stripped and jumped naked into her lap, and she freaked and started chanting Hail Marys, so they buckled to her fervent request to let her out.

on the outskirts they picked up a hitch-hiker from a commune, Kathy Ibrahim.

"We got along with hippies," Ron said. They were all a part of the same subculture. But the drunken bikers were too rowdy for Kathy's sensibilities. Ron stripped and jumped naked into her lap, and she freaked and started chanting Hail Marys, so they buckled to her fervent request to let her out.

At a burned-out gas station and curio shop, Ron and the gang pulled off the freeway to take a leak. Digging through the charred debris, they discovered a pair of steer horns mounted on a plaque. Doc wanted to attach them to his chopper handlebars and threw them in the van.

Just up the road they picked up two male hitchhikers and offered them a beer. When they caught one of their guests stealing brews, Art Smith pulled Doc's .22-caliber pistol out of the glove box and threatened the thieves. Spinning the gun in the old-fashioned Western style, it went off and clipped one of the hitchhiker's ears. Doc was pissed, but they cleaned up the kid and discussed hauling him to a hospital. But because it was just a flesh wound, they dropped the two off on a deserted stretch of Texas highway to allow the Vagos time to escape, in case the hitchhikers filed a complaint.

They made it to Oklahoma before the cops pulled them over. The hitchhikers had filed armed robbery charges against the bikers even though they only took $1 from the hitchhiker for the beer he stole, and charges from Kathy Ibrahim were pending. The group spent the next five days in a Weatherford, Oklahoma jail. They thought it was a joke. When Ron was afforded his required phone call, he ordered a pizza, for which the cop smacked him with the receiver. Their only concern at the time was making the mandatory Vagos meeting on the 15th.

During their stay in the Oklahoma jail, on February 12 a crow hunter discovered the castrated corpse of a transient college student roughly concealed under sage brush in a Tijeras Canyon gully. The outlaws were immediately charged with the brutal murder. The kid, William Velten from South Carolina, was shot in the mouth once. He fell back to the ground and while he pleaded for mercy, his assailant shot him four times in the head, slashed his chest with a knife, cut off his dick, shoved it in his mouth, and sodomized the dying kid.

> Spinning the gun in the old-fashioned Western style, it went off and clipped one of the hitchhiker's ears.

The sheriff's office panicked and immediately convinced magistrate James O'Toole to sign five warrants for the Vagos on March 12, 1974. Bond was set at $100,000 each for Ronald Bruce (Grubby) Keine, Arthur Ray Smith, Thomas Victor Gladish (Ten Speed), and Richard Wayne Greer (alias Orlando Peter Dilda). Orlando was also charged with armed robbery in Tucumcari, New Mexico.

On February 15, the Vagos were extradited to Tucumcari and incarcerated in the Quay County jail, the county where the hitchhikers and Kathy Ibrahim had filed charges. Bernalillo County Sheriff Lester Hay told the press on February 16 that they were good suspects, after deputies Robert Tena and Gilbert Candelaria drove to Tucumcari to interview the bikers. The article in the *Albuquerque Tribune* told of bikers with guns and knives who threatened the Tucumcari service station attendant, who claimed they threatened him, saying "We'll cut you up like we did that guy back in Albuquerque." The quote was a distortion from a hitchhiker's statement. The bikers admitted to taking the steer horns from the charred curio shop remains, but they couldn't figure out why the cops were making such a big deal out of it.

Sheriff Lester Hay stated he had a pretty young female eyewitness, Judith Frances Weyer, under wraps, who was in fear for her life from the Vagos. She was the hotel maid where Velten was supposedly killed.

It was a time of unbalanced power struggles. Small town authorities became over-confident, over-zealous, and believed they had the moral authority to make life and death decisions because they could and should for the good of the community. Communities were shifting under the long white noses of stuffed shirts, crisp ties, and pressed suits. Hippies smoked dope, painted desert landscapes, made macramé displays, and relished in the cultures of the indigenous Indians. The whitebread rule was rapidly losing its righteous popularity. The establishment needed this case to prove that grubby bikers and hippies were trouble and required control.

Officer James Boman questioned the maid, who insisted she didn't know anything about the murder, but gradually her story changed. It was a tough time in her life. She was estranged from her husband and had lost custody of her children. The detectives made her feel critical to the case, supplied her with information, and her story began to fall into place. On March 13, first-degree murder charges were filed against the bikers, and they were transported to the Bernalillo County Jail in Albuquerque.

> He fell back to the ground and while he pleaded for mercy, his assailant shot him four times in the head, slashed his chest with a knife, cut off his dick, shoved it in his mouth, and sodomized the dying kid.

"We figured any day now they were going to let us go," said Ron. They had no idea they were murder suspects. "It was a whole lot of shit for that Kathy chick and the hitchhikers we took a dollar from."

When the bikers found out what they were up against, they quickly reached out to their club brothers in California. The Vagos sent a club attorney, Allan Well of Redondo Beach. Because he wasn't licensed in New Mexico, he hired an Albuquerque attorney, Ron Ginsburg, to serve as co-counsel. Although the maid's testimony was shot full of holes and contradictions, she succeeded in convincing the grand jury. On March 20, less than a week after finding out they were murder suspects, the five Vagos were indicted. District Judge William Riordan set the trial date for May 6. The bikers were whisked off to the New Mexico State Penitentiary.

"They are dangerous and we don't want to take a chance," Sheriff Hay said in a public statement.

"They were trying to intimidate us," Ron said, "to break us down, hoping maybe one of us would confess."

They kept the prisoners separated and away from any form of communication. Even the attorneys had limited access. They were forced to drive to Santa Fe and wait for half a day to meet with a client. Even the attorneys' letters were opened.

"It was a violation of attorney-client privilege for the prison to open our mail," Ron said, "but they did it anyway."

On March 20th, less than a week after finding out they were murder suspects, the five Vagos were indicted.

A number of critical case elements never made the news. In mid-April a thirteen-year-old boy discovered a .22-caliber Ivor Johnson pistol in the arroyo not far from where Velten's body was found, nowhere near the Bel Air Motel. Ballistics tests by the State Police Crime Laboratory proved conclusively that the fatal bullets never came from the bikers' revolvers. Meanwhile, assistant district attorney Brian Gross and his team of sheriff's deputies rehearsed Judy, the maid witness, sometimes eight or nine hours a day. They busted her boyfriend, Jose Rivera, and used him to entice her to testify against the bikers, even promising to help her obtain custody of her kids, put her through secretarial school, and provide assistance until she could get a better job. They promised her the moon but only kept one promise; they held her in protective custody, where the press and the defense attorneys were denied access to her.

They locked Jose down in the same prison with the Vagos. He was assigned the duty of picking up trash in the yard. One day an object smacked Ron's cell bars. It was a granite stone wrapped inside an old, discarded sock.

"I grabbed it, and there was a note inside," Ron said. "After I read it, I passed it around to the other guys. The note said Judy Weyer was lying. She hadn't seen the murder and didn't know anything about it. The note was signed by Jose Rivera."

The original trial date was May 6, and then it was postponed until May 20. In the meantime, sheriff's deputies contacted a young woman who stayed at the Bel Air from February 7 until March 4. Shelley Fish, sixteen, had moved to Maryland with her husband, a Marine sergeant. She was asked to fly out, at the court's expense, to identify photos of the bikers, and was promised that it would take one day, at the most.

Shelley remembered meeting five surfers from California who registered at the motel under the alias Mr. and Mrs. Butts. The surfers stayed in room 45. That was supposedly the location of the Velten murder.

"Weyer claimed she watched Ronald Bruce, "cut and carve on the victim's chest."

Shelley flew out, took one look at the photos of the bikers and the van, and told the investigator she didn't know them and never saw them before. They accused her of lying. The cops questioned her for several days and took her return flight ticket away. Her husband tried to call her, but authorities wouldn't allow him to talk to his wife. He threatened to take legal action against the Bernalillo County Sheriff's Department, and after two weeks of questioning, officers drove her back to the airport, with strident instructions not to discuss the case with anyone.

On May 21, the twenty-seven-year-old Bel Air Motel maid testified at the trial of the five Vagos. Judith Frances Weyer claimed she watched Ronald Bruce, "cut and carve on the victim's chest." She stated on the stand that she saw the Vagos torture the young Velten. "I saw Greer shoot the victim through the head with a gun and then hand the gun to Gladish, who shot him four times."

During the second day of the trial, she testified that the victim was tied with one arm to the bed and the other arm to a chair.

"He was gagged with a towel from the motel," she said. One of the Vagos (Clarence Smith), she continued, " . . . held me about three feet from the victim and made me watch the cutting."

The case shifted just seven days into testimony and Arthur Ray Smith was acquitted, although the polygraph expert said Smith lied when he denied knowledge of the killing. District Court Judge William Riordan ordered the trial to proceed for the other four as the prosecution rested its case. Defense attorneys Ronald Ginsburg, Alice Hector, Allen Well, and Hank Farrah told the *Albuquerque Tribune*, "One down four to go."

Unfortunately the case didn't turn in a positive direction for the other four.

Terry brought a John Wayne-style of violent stability, coupled with a bottomless notion of family, to his growing leadership style in the San Gabriel Chapter in California. By then, Terry had accepted the role as vice president of the San Gabriel Chapter. His abusive childhood brought out a fervent need to protect his brothers.

To fight the case and pay the attorneys, Terry's club was forced to organize, sell bikes, hold auctions, and mortgage homes. They hired an investigator, and Sandman's folks sold their home. But their efforts were to no avail.

On May 31, 1974, Judge Riordan had the jury bused to the Bel Air Motel to view the alleged crime scene at the shabby, bungalow-built, stucco dive surrounded by sand and tumbleweed. The police had stripped room 45 bare. There wasn't a stitch of furniture inside the bare walls, and no floor covering existed. The jury members were not allowed to speak to the motel owner, Nila Baer.

> Terry brought a John Wayne-style of violent stability, coupled with a bottomless notion of family, to his growing leadership style in the San Gabriel Chapter in California.

The acquitted Vago, Arthur Ray Smith, testified that the Michigan-bound Vagos never stopped in Albuquerque. "We never stopped in Albuquerque, never saw the Bel Air Motel and never met William Velten Jr." he said.

Velten's body was found in an arroyo in the Sandia foothills, more than ten miles north of Central Avenue, and time-of-death estimates came in at February 8. The body was badly mutilated and emasculated.

Smith was called back as a defense witness.

"We were in Los Angeles on February 8th," he said. "We were drinking beer and working on a motorcycle."

The defense used gas station credit card receipts to show their whereabouts on February 8 and 9.

"That night in West Covina, Grubby snatched an open container ticket with me," Terry said. "We were out drinking at the Lost Inn, then at Jerry the Jew's bar in Covina. Grubby was driving an old Cadillac and being a jackass. There were four of us in the car when we were pulled over."

But stories didn't connect. Arthur Ray Smith still faced charges of burglary, larceny, and false imprisonment. According to district attorney Brian M. Gross, he broke into the burned-out John Henry Restaurant and Curio Shop in Tijeras Canyon, 200 miles east of Albuquerque.

The cops and the district attorney were anxious for a quick conviction and recruited Jose Antonio of El Paso. He was awaiting trial on charges of rape and contributing to the delinquency of a minor.

"I never saw those defendants before, but the district attorney's office threatened me with charges if I didn't talk for them," Jose said. "Things would be arranged so my charges would be dropped," if he testified that the defendants were in the Bel Air on a particular date.

The trial was rough, but they had alibi witnesses and proof of their activities on February 8 and 9. The only evidence against them was Judy Weyer's testimony, and it was weak and disheveled. They all believed they would be found innocent.

Terry's brothers were hastily convicted of first-degree murder on June 5 and sentenced to die in the New Mexico gas chamber.

Although no real evidence connected the bikers to the crime, it was an election year. The political climate in the small, conservative town demanded a hanging, and the Vagos stumbled into the noose.

☠

Death Row

TERRY HAD JUST TASTED THE MOST BITTER PILL of his life. At twenty-seven, four of his club brothers were on death row, wars with other clubs were ongoing, disputes continued within the Vagos organization, and violence lurked beyond every turn. Toughing it out on the streets with his minimal education was a roll of the dice at best. As quickly as he faced a new situation, society changed and laws changed. He grappled with raising his son, Boomer, as a single dad, running and learning club business, and trying to keep his home together while surrounded in a blanket of turmoil.

The convicted Vagos's execution was set for August 1974. As of 2010, capital judgments were appealed automatically and execution dates would not be etched in iron until after the appeal, but not in 1974. The New Mexico death penalty law had been rescinded in 1972, but it was replaced by a new capital-punishment law presumed to guarantee unbiased application of the death penalty by making execution mandatory for all first-degree murder convictions.

Ten days before the Vagos were scheduled to die, the assistant warden asked Ron about his last meal and any other final requests.

This case tested the constitutionality of the new law. If it had not been challenged on constitutional grounds, the then-recently reinstated New Mexico death penalty statute would be construed as having received the U.S. Supreme Court's seal of approval.

The four brothers sat on death row in the New Mexico State Penitentiary. They were kept in an area nicknamed the Dungeon Hole, a punishment chamber at the prison. Problem inmates were stripped naked and left for days in the darkness there, in solitary confinement, with only a hole in the floor for a toilet.

Ten days before the Vagos were scheduled to die, the assistant warden asked Ron about his last meal and any other final requests.

"I want to hold your hand when they place me in the gas chamber and drop the pellets," he replied.

"I was being a smartass," Ron said. "I made a pledge that I wasn't going to make it easy for them."

Nine days before their scheduled rendezvous with the cyanide gas pellets, their attorneys filed an appeal. They asked for a new trial, citing the judge's failure to sequester the jury and prejudicial pretrial publicity.

"That stayed our execution, temporarily," Ron said. "They couldn't kill us until the court ruled on the appeal."

The system continued to try to break the brothers down. Prison guards beat them, prevented them from sending or receiving any form of communication, and the assistant district attorney promised that if any of them fingered the others, he would be set free. Doc started to lose it.

"He blamed the whole incident on us," said Ron.

Sandman was coming apart, and his tears stained his many letters to his girlfriend.

A trustee strolled past their cells and whispered, "Gross said to tell you, if you're ready to talk, drop him a kite."

Fortunately two reporters from the *Detroit News* started snooping around. When one of Doc's former girlfriends contacted the paper about the case, the paper took a personal interest.

The newspaper received additional complaints from Detroit residents. The paper's managing editor, Boyd Simmons, assigned two reporters to the case: Stephen Cain and Douglas Glazier. Albuquerque authorities wouldn't help; they denied Glazier access to documents and ran him out of town. He returned and checked into a different motel.

The appeal date was moved until January of 1975, and on the 27th of that month the death sentences were stayed pending an appeal to the Supreme Court. Sgt. Donald Heavner, liaison for the district attorney, tried to question Judy Weyer, but he'd lost contact with her. The attorney for the brothers, Hank Farrah, said Weyer was key to their new trial and the only witness scheduled to testify. He also told the local paper that Jim Bowman, a former Albuquerque Police Department officer, might come forward in defense of the Vagos.

Heavner tried to call her repeatedly and sent her threatening news clippings, one about a girl's body discovered in the mountains near Albuquerque.

Detroit News reporter Stephen Cain found Judy Weyer in Minnesota. She had reunited with her husband and four children and was expecting another child. She was reluctant to talk to anyone. Heavner tried to call her repeatedly and sent her threatening news clippings, one about a girl's body discovered in the mountains near Albuquerque.

Judy was scared, but Cain cut a deal with her to tell him the truth. In a series of taped interviews, Judith spoke of the marathon interview sessions and the incessant trial coaching. Cain's *Detroit News* story broke on December 12, 1974. Additional weekly stories were published well into 1975. Judy recanted her entire testimony, and admitted that she had never seen William Velten until she was shown the police photographs. On January 27, the appellate defense team filed a special petition requesting a new trial.

This became a case of bad authorities against innocent bikers who would not give up. The sheriff's department went bad, then the district attorney's office, followed by Judge Riordan, who ultimately turned the case over to Judge H. Verne Payne. And then there was the harsh prison system.

In a letter to the *Detroit News* reporters, Ron said, "The prison apparently isn't letting you see us for two reasons. One, the prison here seems to be working with the D.A. and has openly aborted previous attempts by us to get help to prove our innocence. Two, the prison is afraid we will disclose the way we are being treated here and the conditions of our confinement."

Subsequently Ron was beaten by guards with leather bags full of lead pellets, and he couldn't walk for two weeks. Terry, the young leader in California, quickly learned that the most cold-blooded, fiendish crimes were inflicted by authorities gone bad.

On March 31, 1975, a headline on the front page of the *Albuquerque Tribune* read, "I Lied, Star Witness Sobs." While bawling her eyes out Judith testified, "I couldn't live with the big lie anymore. I was not present when William Velten was killed. I don't know who killed him."

> Subsequently Ron was beaten by guards with leather bags full of lead pellets, and he couldn't walk for two weeks.

She was told not to testify by her attorney, C.A. Bowerman, because she could be criminally prosecuted for perjury, but she insisted. The local cops had forced her to testify against the Vagos, she said. They used every immoral means possible, from bribery to extortion.

"They kept after me," Judy said. "They kept putting things in my mouth. They went on and on," until she testified for the prosecution. The audacity of authorities to take justice into their own hands had reached criminal levels.

She told the paper that she was interviewed by the police, "almost every day, constantly, sometimes for eight or nine hours. They (the officers) told me they knew for sure the defendants did it."

But was that the case? The cops told her they would regain custody of her kids if she testified for the prosecution.

During the March appeal hearing, she testified that she didn't witness the murder. "They laughed at me," she said. She also told the court about her erroneous personal injury testimony during the previous trial. She wasn't cut under her breasts by the outlaws or raped by them.

Another twist surfaced while the brothers sat on death row. An inmate at the New Mexico state pen testified on April 2 about his homosexual lover. According to Eugene Greer, who was serving time for robbery in western New Mexico, I.D. Bickford claimed he had killed Velten, and he had described the murder while the two occupied adjoining cells.

The testimony surfaced in front of District Judge William Riordan on the third day of a hearing for a new trial. The attorneys for the defense based their case for a new trial on Greer's statements and the recantation of Judy Weyer, the only supposed eyewitness.

Unfortunately, during questioning by District Attorney James L. Brandenburg, Greer admitted speaking to one of the convicted men through a vent at the penitentiary. The judged denied a new trial, and then turned the case over to Judge Payne.

"After re-reading the trial testimony and reviewing the testimony at this hearing," said the judge, "I have come to the conclusion that Mrs. Weyer perjured herself at this hearing when she said she did not witness the killing of William Velten Jr. by the defendants."

The brothers were once more placed on death row while the slippery wheels of justice turned in reverse. ☠

The Missing Link

IN SEPTEMBER OF 1975, A TWENTY-FIVE-YEAR-OLD, hot-shot gigolo from Rome, California, who was headed for Florida ran out of money in North Charleston, South Carolina.

At one over-confident time, he had professed of unending sexual prowess.

"I can seduce any man or woman I want," Kerry Lee said.

But he wasn't brimming with arrogance when he stepped into the Charleston Heights Baptist Church's home for young wanderers. While speaking to a minister, he was overcome with the need to clear his conscience. He told the minister about killing a man. The minister encouraged him to speak to the police, Kerry Lee agreed, and he confessed to the murder of William Velten. According to Kerry Rodney Lee, it was a drug deal gone bad.

Prior to the summer of 1975, Lee was never a figure in this case. The four young brothers on death row never heard of Lee, didn't know him, and never met the tall, narrow kid who could save their lives.

Hank Farrah and Vince D'Angelo immediately jumped at the chance to pull their clients off death row, but district attorney Brandenburg fought them at every turn.

"There's not one piece of evidence that ties Lee to Velten," Brandenburg argued.

The minister encouraged him to speak to the police, Kerry Lee agreed, and he confessed to the murder of William Velten. According to Kerry Rodney Lee, it was a drug deal gone bad.

Although Brandenburg ardently supported the conviction, a series of affidavits from Lee surfaced. The car used by Lee was towed from the area where Velten's body was discovered on February 6, proving that Lee was obviously in the vicinity of the murder at the time.

The tow truck driver, Patricio Antonio Gonzales, stated in an affidavit that he did pull a car out of the area at about 2:20 a.m. on February 6. The driver was Lee, Gonzales confirmed. A local police officer, Patrick O'Hearn, admitted that he assisted Lee in towing the car out of the arroyo the same night.

Lee's girlfriend established that Lee did have the car that night, although her name was withheld by the authorities. She discovered a Western Skies receipt in the car. She said Lee, "told me that he had killed a guy and referred to the night that he stayed at the Western Skies."

The gun used in the crime was discovered missing from the girlfriend's father's gun cabinet. The gun was recovered a half-mile from the location of Velten's body on April 28, 1974, by some children walking in the area.

Authorities discovered a bullet hole in Lee's car, matching Lee's statement that the car was struck by a bullet during the fight. The bullet was matched to the gun found near the scene. Lee even claimed he rented a metal detector to search for the gun, and the rental store had a receipt for the detector signed by Lee.

From the standpoint of the defense attorneys, the case was unraveling before their eyes. But Brandenburg didn't budge, and the clogged wheels of justice moved very slowly for the four defendants on death row. Finger-pointing and accusations flew within the law enforcement community. Lee claimed he worked for the Independent Order of Foresters, which was confirmed. Lee remained in Albuquerque for about a month after the murder, working for the Foresters.

Affidavits continued to blow holes in the case against the Vagos. It was revealed that Lee called Albuquerque authorities from California after the Vagos were convicted. Richard L. Oliver, Lee's friend in California, signed an affidavit that Lee did call the Bernillo County sheriff's office on September 21 and said that he wanted to confess to a murder. Brandenburg was forced to admit that the sheriff's office did receive the call.

Lee continued to reveal detailed evidence, including drawing a map outlining where the slaying occurred and diagramming his movements. He remembered the area well because he had searched it extensively with the metal detector.

The murder weapon remained the one inconclusive piece of evidence. Ballistics tests attempted to match Lee's gun to the .22-caliber bullets taken from Velten's body.

"The State Police Lab said the bullets were too messed up for an accurate test, but said they could have been fired by the gun, and the gun could be ruled out as the murder weapon," Farrah said.

Brandenburg agreed that the ballistics tests were inconclusive. Unfortunately, one of the guns recovered from the van used by the four Vagos was also a .22-caliber pistol.

Brandenburg publicly grappled with the connection between Velten and Lee. According to Lee, they met only hours before the slaying while transacting a drug deal. Lee refused to incriminate anyone else involved in the marijuana sale.

Hank Farrah never believed the drug deal story, saying, "I think there was another connection."

Brandenburg tried to shoot holes in Lee's testimony, stating that, "there were defense wounds on Velten's hands, indicating he was alive when he was cut, not dead as Lee said."

From the standpoint of the defense attorneys, the case was unraveling before their eyes. But Brandenburg didn't budge, and the clogged wheels of justice moved very slowly for the four defendants on death row.

Brandenburg tried to blame the defense efforts on the *Detroit News*, whose reporters became involved, flew to Albuquerque, and interviewed the cops' star witness, the Bel Air Motel maid.

"The whole prosecutor's case was fabricated," said public defender Hank Farrah. "The Vagos never stopped in Albuquerque." They were arrested in Weatherford, Oklahoma, 60 miles west of Oklahoma City, almost 500 miles from Albuquerque.

But the battle wasn't over.

Another year was just about to slip past when the December 5 *Albuquerque Tribune* headline read, "Defendants Unknown, New Velten Case Trial Set for February 3, 1976." The four bikers were finally granted a new trial. New ballistics evidence indicated that the gun found near the body was linked to the crime.

The four Vagos had spent 17 months on death row. "Are you guilty?" asked staff writer William Gibson.

"No, and that's the first time anybody asked us that question," said Ronald B. Keine. "They just picked us up and stuffed us in jail for something we didn't do."

Lee's confession finally reopened the case. If Lee had never confessed, all four men would have been murdered by the state. Fortunately for them he did confess, and on December 18, 1975, the four were released. Only one of the four Vagos—Ron Keine—is still alive today. Doc ended up in Florida, Flash later hung himself, and Ten-Speed moved to Oregon and later died.

A year after the Vagos' release, a $10 million damages suit was filed in New Mexico claiming that authorities conspired to, and did, manufacture evidence falsely to show the four men killed Velten, committed false testimony, and induced false testimony. After court costs were subtracted from the settlement, the defendants received very little.

The brothers, including Terry, waited for the four men to come home, but only Sandman returned to club life. Keine returned to his home in Detroit and attempted to work with *Detroit News* reporter Douglas Glazier on a book about the case. He built a successful plumbing business and remained in Detroit. A book was written on the case and published in 2008, *Execution's Doorstep*, by Leslie Lytle. The case was just one chapter in a book that compiled sordid tales of authorities and law enforcement gone dreadfully wrong.

Life in Los Angeles moved on at a machine-gun pace. Vago chapters grew. In 1976 Terry became San Gabriel chapter president. San Gabriel, a historic hub of violence, the scene of a pivotal battle in the Mexican-American War (1846-1848). First the Spanish brutalized the American Indians, then the whites took it back from the Mexicans. The brothers didn't realize the historically violent surroundings in which they resided. Club chapters took on personalities of their own. Some sought to be gangsters, some became drug addicts, and others wanted the bully reputation.

And, said Terry, "Some scavenged for bike parts and sat in bars drinking all day."

Terry tried to hold his chapter together as it grew. "Shit was too crazy," he said. "I spent most of my time dealing with one problem after another."

> Doc ended up in Florida, Flash later hung himself, and Ten-Speed moved to Oregon and later died.

☠

The Doctor's Visit

THE PERIOD FROM THE MID- TO LATE 1970S was the toughest stretch for motorcycle clubs. Clubs broke out of the traditional mold of fun-loving, crazed chopper riders and transitioned into bands of thugs and gangsters. Machismo was the guiding force as clubs rumbled from being local bullies into wider competition with other clubs, territorial disputes, gangster antics, and tough-guy notions. It's unfortunate that clubs didn't invent the World Wrestling Federation (known today as World Wrestling Entertainment) and make their disputes an entertaining sport. It would have been far more financially successful and would have prevented decades of jail time. Club life became a dog-eat-dog street world, fueled by barbiturates, marijuana, alcohol, meth, cocaine, and hallucinogenic drugs.

The blood of hate flowed like rivers through the asphalt and concrete streets. As street warriors searched for combat, weapons became badges of honor; beatings and killings became badges of manhood. Brothers hated the government, the media, and their drunken or abusive parents. The lousy Vietnam War scaled down, while Watergate showcased an unimagined level of rampant government corruption. Bikers ran free until the establishment decided to curb their appetite by enacting helmet laws, highbar laws, and loud-pipe restrictions in an effort to reign in the wild chopper hordes.

As the 1970s stormed to a close, every violent gesture peaked like the rush from a mound of cocaine. It was a time of overt violence, like the blade of a knife sharpened constantly until it itched to cut something, anything.

Club life became a dog-eat-dog street world, fueled by barbiturates, marijuana, alcohol, meth, cocaine, and hallucinogenic drugs.

"We lost a whole chapter in Desert Hot Springs," Terry said. According to Terry, "They started out as a good group of guys." But something else came into play over a short period of time. Terry made a point to attend charter meetings from time to time and he noticed a change in the charter located in the notorious Coachella Valley, a fast-growing town in the 1970s. The small desert burgh was noted for its natural hot mineral waters and award-winning municipal drinking water, but something other than water was entering the nervous systems of the local Vagos: speed, or crank.

"I noticed a change in the members' behavior during meetings," Terry said. "They were babbling idiots. They were spending too much time in the fast lane."

The sideways jaw movements, teeth grinding, and shifting eyes gave away their methamphetamine use. At first it increased their alertness, concentration, energy, euphoria, self-esteem, and libido. But the constant use ate at their internal organs, deteriorating teeth, bone structure, appearance, and behavior, resulting in a psychosis resembling schizophrenia. The charter even included a retired California Highway Patrol officer named Danny in the eight- to ten-men ranks. But the tall, thinning Danny became as addicted as the rest, and his ability to become a leader dissipated until the charter fell apart.

"A couple of members retired and turned in their patches," Terry said. "The drug became more important than their motorcycles or the club and they left their shit behind and peeled out."

Then the Man came into play. Cops and bikers clashed. One group sought to control the other, and that wasn't going to happen without a fight. It was the John Wayne straight-arrow against the thug on a metal-flake, chromed-out chopper.

Terry built a new bike from a 1959 Dresser, which he stripped and transformed into a rigid-framed chopper. Every day was a party for many brothers, but Terry worked during the day at the studios and then blasted home to take care of his son and work on his new motorcycle project at night.

One night Terry rolled to the slick new Denny's franchise restaurant on Peck Road in El Monte, where Jinx and Parts were hanging out. Terry sat at the counter and was enjoying his traditional cup of Joe when three young toughs pushed their way into the restaurant.

The three young men were related; two were brothers and one was a cousin. As it turned out, Jinx, who wasn't a fighter but was always willing to start shit, had some past dealings with the three. One of the trio approached Jinx, who was sitting with Parts in a slick linoleum booth. At first he leaned over and said something to Jinx and poked him in the chest with his right index finger. Jinx sat back and mouthed off to the man, feeling safe while surrounded by his Vago brothers. He felt the power of the brotherhood around him, but the troublemaker, recently released from San Quentin, wasn't intimidated by the patches. He pushed Jinx's plate of food into his lap and slapped him in the face. Terry watched and noted a Vago prospect in the corner not doing anything. As it turned out, he was related to the three.

> Cops and bikers clashed. One group sought to control the other, and that wasn't going to happen without a fight. It was the John Wayne straight-arrow against the thug on a metal-flake, chromed-out chopper.

Terry wasn't a big man, but he had a short fuse and zero tolerance for intimidation. He spun off his slick counter stool and came face-to-face with a much larger man.

"That's my brother," Terry said.

Tough Terry the Tramp in the late 1970s in a SGV bar. *Photo copyright © 2011 Silver*

"He's a punk," the intruder said, "and I'm going to fuck him and you up, little man."

The shit was on and Terry beat the bigger man right out the door of the restaurant and into the parking lot. One of the other men returned and threatened the Vagos before leaving.

The Vagos finished dinner and Terry went home to check on his son and take his new chopper out for a break-in ride. He pulled his bike out of the stucco garage located in a small complex of apartments. As he rode it out onto Cherry Lee Street, he noticed a sedan pull into the complex. He didn't like the looks of the guys in the sedan and returned. He rode through the maze of concrete checking for anything out of the ordinary, and then leaned his chopper for Cherry Lee once more. He pulled left out

He pushed Jinx's plate of food into his lap and slapped him in the face.

of the complex and juiced the chopper to the boulevard stop, where he spotted the sedan once more on the right, down the block from the intersecting residential street.

As he snapped the quick throttle and launched the big motor-cycle across the intersection, the dark sedan pulled away from the curb and approached. Gunshots rang out as the car skidded right and approached from the rear. Terry suddenly lost control and his motorcycle went down in the center of the street, but the revolver fire kept coming until the car sped past and disappeared.

A small girl on a Honda motorcycle was the first person on the scene. She was an off-duty police officer and offered to get help. She banged on the nearest residential door. No one answered. She rode home and called the El Monte EMTs.

One small-caliber bullet seared through Terry's left arm, while a second slug lodged near his spine. He was taken immediately to the El Monte hospital, where he squirmed in pain until Parts arrived.

Parts found Terry had been waiting for an extended period without being examined. Parts scoured the halls until he discovered the young emergency room doctors sipping coffee in the staff lounge.

"You better examine my brother," Parts snapped, "or you will be the next in line for care."

The doctor moved quickly, dressed Terry's wounds, ordered X-rays, and gave him a shot of Demerol for the pain. As the pain subsided, cops entered the hospital to investigate the shooting. Terry and Parts slipped out the back of the medical complex and began to kick down doors looking for the shooters.

> Gunshots rang out as the car skidded left and approached from the rear. Terry suddenly lost control and his motorcycle went down in the center of the street.

At 3:00 a.m., the pair stumbled into the Denny's and discovered cops in every booth waiting for them. Officers arrested Terry and took him to the large, foreboding Los Angeles general hospital gunshot ward, where he received more Demerol and then went into surgery.

While Terry was in the gunshot ward, a black man who had been shot by his wife for cheating was admitted. He was examined and then rolled into surgery. An hour passed and he was returned to the bland, sterile ward for recovery. As the nurse worked with him in the large, sanitary quarters, which housed six gunshot victims, a nasty-looking, big black woman appeared. She smiled at the nurse and inquired of her husband's condition.

"Will he make it?" she asked.

"Certainly, ma'am," the nurse said. "He'll be fine."

As the nurse bent over to administer the IV to her husband, the wife pulled the same revolver from her purse that she had used to shoot him the first time, and she shot him again. All hell broke loose in the ward.

The next day Terry rested in the hospital surrounded by Vagos. Parts slipped Terry a loaded, snub-nosed Smith and Wesson .38-caliber revolver. As the brothers discussed Terry's health and healing, the search for the shooter, and the problem that caused the mess, two shooters entered his hospital room.

The large, swinging door rolled open on heavyweight, sprung, stainless-steel hinges. The two gunmen pulled revolvers and began to shoot at anything that moved.

The ward erupted in a gunfight as Vago members grabbed for their weapons and returned fire. The two outmatched shooters ran out the door, chased by four Vagos. They escaped for the time being, but the hunt was in high gear as members of the club chased them as far as Texas.

The three bad-boy relatives finally turned to the law for protection. Unfortunately for them, they were under investigation for another drug-related murder and ultimately did a decade in the penitentiary.

Terry later learned that Jinx had initiated the confrontation by ripping

The Vagos had two rules: No drugs and no faggots. Jinx had broken at least one of those rules and was out of the club.

them off during a drug deal gone bad. The Vagos had two rules: No drugs and no faggots. Jinx had broken at least one of those rules and was out of the club.

Terry sold the new 1959 Panhead chopper to a local rider, who got high and street-raced the motorcycle to his death. He ran a light and collided with a car, which severed his leg. He bled to death. ☠

The Call for Guns

AS THE PRESIDENT OF THE SAN GABRIEL CHAPTER of the Vagos, Terry was on call 24/7. Too often the calls came in the middle of the night.

One night just a few months into 1978, when he still carried a cast on his left arm from being shot off his bike, Terry scrambled out of bed when the phone rang. It was 1:30 in the morning as the moon crept into the warm, smog-soaked sky above teeming Los Angeles city streets.

He heard Parts's tentative voice on the phone. Parts said something about guns, so Terry loaded his 1968 Chevy Impala coupe with shotguns and revolvers and peeled across town for the notorious Denny's all-night diner on Peck Road, the main artery through El Monte into Duarte. Terry recognized trouble as he pulled into the well-lit parking lot and spotted a lowered, jet-black El Camino. It contained a notorious black-haired thug with a full, black beard. It was Black Beard, a local tough guy who didn't like the growing presence of Vagos in his town.

> Black Beard sneered at him and lifted a long-barreled Bulldog .44 magnum, pointing it in Terry's direction.

Terry jumped out of his coupe and strode over to Parts, who faced the short-haired El Camino driver with a stern look. The driver held a sawed-off shotgun in his lap. Terry stuffed a small, .38-caliber snub-nosed revolver in Parts's rear denim pocket and walked around the front of the polished El Camino, sparkling in the asphalt parking lot. As he approached the passenger window, Black Beard sneered at him and lifted a long-barreled Bulldog .44 magnum, pointing it in Terry's direction.

Terry stepped closer and grabbed the big, blued barrel, twisting it toward the dashboard. The cannon went off, taking out the windshield and knocking Terry to the pavement.

All hell broke loose. Parts yanked the snub-nosed revolver from his denims, backed up, and fired into the driver's door. Terry drew and fired his .38, then scrambled to his feet and jumped into the bed of the truck, firing through the rear window. Jerry the Jew peeled into the parking lot in his '57 Chevy and Terry ran around the custom car for cover while drawing fire from the El Camino's cab. Jerry's Chevy took twenty-seven rounds, although Jerry was unarmed and unharmed.

"Did you bring ammo?" Terry hollered at Jerry, who slipped him a quick load. The brothers continued to fire into the El Camino.

Within minutes, a police bullhorn barked from the parking lot across the street. The Vagos wiped their untraceable weapons clean and tossed them aside.

"Who fired the weapons?" officers demanded.

"What weapons?" Terry said. There were no witnesses. Brodie fell out of his side of the car into a pool of his own blood. When asked the identity of the man, Jerry kicked him in the head.

"Never saw him before," he answered.

Terry spit on the wounded Black Beard when questioned. Because there were no witnesses, no charges were filed that night. The two wounded men were hauled to the county hospital, where they survived despite multiple gunshot wounds. A month later, while holding court at 1:00 in the morning at that same Denny's, local law enforcement stormed the restaurant and arrested Terry and Parts, booking them for attempted murder.

When questioned in court, Terry said, "It was the worst case of attempted suicide I've ever run across."

"He's a hostile witness," the district attorney complained to the judge.

All charges were eventually dropped, but the divide between the Vagos and the local authorities was widening.

A year later, while Terry worked on his motorcycle in his garage, a dark figure emerged in the driveway. As the dim light from his garage illuminated the visitor's face, Terry reached for a ball peen hammer and spun to meet Black Beard's brother.

"It's okay," the kid said, raising his hands. "Why didn't you kill him?"

Not long after the shootout, Terry found himself drinking at the Nashville Bar in El Monte on a Friday night. Friday was the most light-hearted night of the weekend. As weekends rolled on and the booze and Seconal flowed, attitudes reached a sharper edge.

Terry was feeling no pain as he started to mess with a new blonde babe at the bar. They danced to the jukebox-delivered country-western tunes and played grab-ass until a clean-cut drunk approached Terry.

"You need to find another girl to fool with," he said, attitude written all over his slick, clean-shaven face. "She came with me."

"You need to find another girl to fool with," he said, attitude written all over his slick, clean-shaven face. "She came with me."

"Did you come with this idiot?" Terry asked the girl.

"No," she said with a smirk.

"Looks like you've got a problem, punk," Terry said, and the fight was on. Terry immediately sized his opponent up and tried to strike him in the neck, but this similar-sized man had training and blocked Terry's initial blow. They fought across the bar and outside the restaurant into the parking lot. At one time, the man's pistol came loose from his lower back holster and fell to the pavement. Terry looked for an inside shot below his ribs.

"A good body shot drops 'em every time," Terry said.

Cops were called and Terry could hear sirens in the distance closing on the biker bar. A friend, Frenchie, peeled into the parking lot in his new silver 1980 Firebird and screamed, "Get in! The cops are coming!"

Terry jumped in the Firebird and Frenchie peeled north on Peck towards Garvey at more than 100 mph. They blew through an intersection where the road split and the car nearly rolled out of control.

"Slow down," Terry said. "Are your trying to kill us?"

The cops were on their tail and there was nowhere to run in the foothills. Finally, Terry convinced the big Canadian to pull over, and cops immediately surrounded the car.

"You're going down for this one," the lead officer snapped at the driver.

"You can't take Frenchie," Terry said. "He was cool. I reached across and jammed his foot against the gas pedal."

The cops cut Frenchie loose and the Tramp was booked at the El Monte Police department for assault on a police officer. Parts bailed him out with $250. The arresting officer approached Terry outside the El Monte courtroom.

"You know the guy you fought was a cop?" He said.

"So that's why he could fight," Terry said.

"Are you looking to die?" Terry asked.

Later that night, Terry and Parts sipped hot mugs of coffee at their Denny's restaurant hangout. He pondered the new charge against his sour record. The coffee shop became more than his office. He often pulled cash from the till to bail out brothers.

"We always returned it," Terry said.

Later that night, the cop he fought earlier entered the coffee shop.

"Are you looking to die?" Terry asked.

"I didn't come to fight again," the officer said. "It was just a fight, no hard feelings."

"But I was arrested and it cost me $250 to get the hell out of jail," Terry said.

"I'll take care of it," the officer said, paid him the $250, and the charges were dropped. Terry recognized solid cops, yet the rift between the Man and the growing number of Vagos in the city was widening, like bad blood in a family. ☠

Vagos vs. the City of El Monte

WHEN RICHARD NIXON RAN FOR PRESIDENT in 1968, he promised to restore American values. Like damned near every other asshole running for that office, he meant the opposite of what he said. What he really meant—and most people understood this and supported it—was that he was going to gut the hippy movement and destroy the filthy, subversive longhairs who were scaring the shit out of the general public. The Vietnam riots, helmet-law protests, and student uprisings motivated government response against what vice president Spiro Agnew labeled the "effete corps of impudent snobs."

The government's philosophy and actions ran directly counter to real American values. The United States had been settled by immigrants seeking freedom, and its people value freedom as the most American of principles. What Nixon set out to do, and in many ways succeeded in doing, was destroying our freedom,

Though they shared little common ideology with the hippies, one-percenters were lumped into the same free-wheeling category as far as law enforcement was concerned, and bikers were a much juicier target.

with the help of his corrupt Attorney General John Mitchell, who served nineteen months in prison for engineering the infamous burglaries at the Watergate Hotel.

But before Nixon resigned in disgrace and Mitchell was sent to a federal pound-me-up-the-ass prison, the pair managed to unleash law-enforcement agencies across the country in a violent, knee-jerk reaction to the hippy movement. Part of this attack against the counterculture involved equipping law enforcement agencies with the latest and greatest weaponry and surveillance technology. Though they shared little common ideology with the hippies, one-percenters were lumped into the same free-wheeling category as far as law enforcement was concerned, and bikers were a much juicier target. Any competitive edge the one-percenters might have had in earlier years was nullified by the increased scrutiny from enhanced capabilities of law enforcement.

The brothers survived the 1960s and hung onto their freedom, but only by the most tenuous thread; growing government entities spent formidable budgets researching enforcement technology and devious ways to pass legislation to control more segments of the population in increasingly formidable ways.

The government's philosophy and actions ran directly counter to real American values. The United States had been settled by immigrants seeking freedom, and its people value freedom as the most American of principles.

Protests across the country beat back the initial wave of helmet laws, but NHTSA and the unforgiving Department of Transportation (DOT) didn't give up their control-freak, budget-expanding extortion tactics. They conjured up the Public Burden Theory and suddenly the black plague of helmet laws slit the throat of freedom once again. Without warning, anyone injured on a motorcycle was branded a tax burden to the public, at least according to the media and much to the chagrin of the freedom-loving motorcyclist population.

The federal government leaned on states to pass helmet laws by threatening to withhold highway funds. The nefarious tactic was successful and forced several states to enact more restrictive legislation.

In 1974, Don Pittsley, a member of the Huns MC in Bridgeport, Connecticut, persuaded his congressman, Representative Stewart McKinney, to introduce H.R. 3869 in the U.S. Congress. This bill would end the federal authority to withhold highway funds from states that failed to enact helmet laws. Before 1975 ended, committee chairman Senator Jesse Helms added the language of H.R. 3869 to the 1975 Federal Highway Act. It became known as the "Helms Angel Bill" and on May 5, 1976, President Gerald Ford signed it into law. It was nothing short of miraculous that a tiny number of concerned bikers could affect federal law.

"They started jacking us up and writing tickets for bullshit reasons, like leaving our keys in the ignitions," Terry said. "They were looking for a beef and they got it."

Unfortunately, it didn't end helmet laws.

The Vagos still lived in the 1960s, at least in their own minds. They refused to accept the increasing restrictions that a growing government presence was pushing on them. They still acted like they lived in a world where a brother could outrun the cops and return to laugh about it. Law enforcement felt the unrelenting pressure from city fathers to deal with unruly one-percenters still roaming the streets unbridled. There was also a growing competitive edge within various law enforcement agencies, and they began arresting bikers almost as a competitive sport.

El Monte was an incorporated city within Los Angeles County, with its own police force, but portions of Duarte, another unincorporated community, were patrolled by LA Sheriffs, and LA City Police controlled other areas. Like football teams, they reviewed and mocked each others' bad arrest scores.

Cops became more aggressive, initiating busts and outright attacks on Vagos members, such as the out-and-out assault on the

Boot Hill Saloon at Peck and Durfee streets in El Monte, a typical local dive with peanut shells scattered on the concrete deck. This happened one particular Los Angeles night under a full moon.

"They started jacking us up and writing tickets for bullshit reasons, like leaving our keys in the ignitions," Terry said. "They were looking for a beef and they got it."

Gary Robels, a Hell's Angel, was with the Vagos that night.

"He tore up his ticket and threw it at the cops," Terry said. "It took six of them to wrestle Gary into a cop car."

They kicked Kickback Billy, who was knocked to the ground during the scuffle, and two officers wrestled Terry into a patrol car.

Every weekend it became tougher for Vagos to party openly in the streets, but they remained defiant. Shortly after the Boot Hill incident, several Vagos ran into a group of drunken, off-duty LAPD detectives in the Nashville West bar. While Jinx and Breakdown Billy played pool in a dark corner of the rustic bar, the cops did shooters and bad-mouthed the bikers. Finally around 1:00 a.m. Jinx recognized the impending confrontation. He slipped out of through the back door exit and across the dark parking lot to a phone booth in the gas station across the street to call for biker back-up.

Breakdown Billy and another member confronted the unruly cops and the conflict moved outside into the oil-soaked parking lot, where the undercover cops went to blows with the Vagos. One cop spotted Jinx in the phone booth across the lot and shot him. Another officer in a plain-clothes city-official sedan ran over Breakdown Billy.

Uniformed officers were called, and the drunken officers from Temple City peeled out. The parking lot swarmed with police cars and emergency vehicles. The bad cops returned, this time in an official capacity.

At 7:00 a.m., during the investigation, the undercover officers were required to blow into breathalyzers, and they all still

> At 7:00 a.m., during the investigation, the undercover officers were required to blow into breathalyzers, and they all still reported drunk.

reported drunk. The case took more than two years to be completed. Jinx, who survived the gunshot wound, was paid handsomely. Terry learned that the Man could be beaten at his own game.

One evening while one of Terry's stepsisters was working at Denny's as a waitress, Terry gave her $2,500 in a crumpled brown paper bag.

"Return this to the boss," Terry said. "We needed some bail money."

She was on duty, so she shoved the bag deep into a Formica shelf below the cash register. The stiff-shirt boss went ballistic when he discovered the short take for the night.

"What would it take for you guys to go somewhere else for a week so I can sell this place?" Shortly thereafter, behind numerous complaints, late-night fights, loud motorcycles, and trouble with the law, the restaurant closed.

Terry relocated his office to another all-night diner, Sambo's restaurant in El Monte. On another weekend night, a unit of LAPD special assignment officers surrounded the 24-hour coffee shop and prepared for an assault on the two Vago leaders and any other members of the green team they could find. They dragged Terry, Parts, and Breakdown Billy into the asphalt parking lot, where they beat them with batons and heavy flashlights, splitting Parts' skull open.

"I was hot," Terry said. Beaten and bruised, he rode across town to the Billiard Den, a dark pool hall. He ducked inside the late-night hangout for coffee, smokes, and general peace, but he was confronted by a plain-clothes Los Angeles County Sheriff's deputy. The cop immediately got in the Tramp's face.

"Shut up, you fuckin' punk," Terry told the cop, who was about his size. "He was the shortest sheriff I had ever seen."

"Look, you puke," he said to Terry. "We are taking you guys down."

"Lose the gun and badge, and we can handle this man-to-man," Terry said. The officer agreed and the two men marched out back and threw blows on the soiled asphalt.

"He had guts," Terry said. "He kicked my ass."

"We ended up in another two-year lawsuit over that special unit case," Terry continued. They ultimately dropped the case and the LA Sheriff dropped all charges.

The tangled web of distrust, hatred, social divisions, and criminal activity on both sides of the law reached a fevered pitch. It was a battle to see who would survive, but as always, the cops played with a marked deck.

As Terry tried to hold his family life together during the constant turmoil, he came to a crossroads with his personal behavior. He didn't do drugs but he drank with the worst of them. One night playing pool at the Boot Hill, he struck up a game with a giant of a man who played with a vengeance. With each loss, the big man became more incensed. After the third defeat, he snapped a .38 out of a shoulder holster and stuck it in Terry's face.

"I'm going to blow your fuckin' head off," the big bastard spat.

"Not tonight you're not," Terry said. He pushed the gun aside and hit him three times with a cue ball. Then several of his brother Vagos jumped into the melee.

> "Lose the gun and badge, and we can handle this man-to-man," Terry said. The officer agreed and the two men marched out back of the all-night diner and threw blows.

Terry was approaching a junction. Life was all about choices. One too many drunken gun battles, knife fights, or wild rides, and the dice would eventually come up snake eyes. He would end up dead or in prison. He was the president of SGV, and his brothers relied on him to make smart, canny, and thoughtful decisions. He watched too many brothers take inebriated falls, die in accidents, or go to jail over stupid shit. He had to have both feet planted on solid turf. ☠

Trickbags and Sting Operations

FOR A WHILE IT WAS ALL ABOUT BEING TOUGH, guarding Vagos' territories, and building a hollow reputation that wasn't vacant. The Vagos ran to LA, Little Rock, and into the South Bay. For a while, they hit Long Beach on weekends. One weekend while partying with a group of Sundowners out of Ogden, Utah, they wrecked four saloons before the Long Beach Police Department surrounded them in the fourth bar.

Terry and Fonzy slipped out the back of the bar with their girls and escaped to one of the babe's houses nearby. In her car, they returned to witness all their brothers sprawled in the seaside street. They were all arrested and their motorcycles were impounded.

Dale, left, Monster Red, and Randy roaming the vendor-packed parking lots during the annual Laughlin River Run at the Colorado Belle Casino Hotel.

One weekend while partying with a group of Sundowners out of Ogden, Utah, they wrecked four saloons before the Long Beach Police Department surrounded them in the fourth bar.

Late one Sunday night they ran in a pack of 20 riders out to San Bernardino to party with another chapter. On the trip out to Berdoo, they flew down Interstate 10 in the fast lane, flying out of the city with chrome sparkling and pipes blasting into the night sky.

Suddenly out of nowhere, a foreign compact car weaved into their lane and split the pack just behind Terry's rear wheel. At seventy-five mph, the group of motorcycles went down like dominos. The driver swerved out of the collision and tried to run, but Terry and a brother, Randy, were still upright and gave chase for over two miles, trying to force the drunken driver off the freeway.

Bashing the side of the compact with their fists, the driver finally acquiesced and slowed, pulling into the asphalt emergency lane. A CHP unit skidded to a stop behind Terry, siren blasting and lights flashing. Then another black and white sped to the scene. Terry and Randy worried that if they jumped off their bikes and moved away from the compact, the drunk might escape. The officers moved on the bikers and not the driver, as if they were attacking an unsuspecting motorist.

"He crashed into our pack!" Terry barked.

"Step away from the car," the officer ordered.

"You don't get it!" Terry said.

The argument continued until a radio report caught the officer's attention. Several motorcycles were knocked down in the fast lane two miles back. The small Asian man in the bruised compact car could hardly stand when he was removed and consequently arrested for a DUI and reckless driving.

Every night, it was something. But it wasn't always the man against unfortunate, innocent clubbers.

"We were building a sour reputation," Terry said. "If a guy made the mistake of hanging with us, he usually lost his motorcycle or got his ass kicked."

The Vagos ran amok every night. At the time, one-percenter club members messed with anyone who came around. And, said Terry, "When we weren't fuckin' with outsiders or other clubs, we attacked each other."

At seventy-five mph, the group of motorcycles went down like dominos.

One such occurrence in December of 1979 turned seriously nasty when Igor, a member of the Cossacks MC, tried to party with the Scavengers. His motorcycle was stripped from his possession and he was sent down the road, beaten badly. The next day, Vago members reached out to Igor and offered to return his chopper for $500, but Igor had contacted law enforcement, and a sting operation was set in motion.

Los Angeles Police Detective Michael Lane, thirty-one, working undercover as a biker club member, was an eleven-year veteran in the department. He took Igor to P.J.'s Cocktail Lounge on Whittier Boulevard and set up a meeting in an open parking lot across the street. It was a trap and the Vagos knew it.

Rocky Lee Berch, twenty-seven, a member of the Scavengers MC, was a bad-ass, more than willing to build a desperado reputation within the Vago ranks. He grabbed a new Vago member, George Harvey, twenty-eight, of Rohnert Park near Santa Rosa, as backup. He was a thick muscled kid, five-foot eight-inches tall, with long, wavy brown hair and a full beard. He rode an old Panhead and worked hard in the oil fields.

As they approached a Toyota pickup to meet with Igor, Detective Lane stepped out hoisting a sawed off shotgun and all hell broke loose. Rocky unloaded his pistol. George pulled his new, unloaded gun tucked in his lower back waistband, but he was knocked to the ground by fire from surrounding cops, who were hiding behind other vehicles and shrubbery. The windshield was blown out and Detective Lane died of multiple gun shot wounds, whereas the six-foot ten-inch Igor didn't suffer a scratch.

"I never could figure this one out," Terry said. "The cop was riddled, Igor wasn't touched, and the two brothers were hit several times."

Rocky died at the scene and George lay in a pool of blood for more than an hour before he was taken to the hospital.

"They wanted him to die," Terry said. Once dragged into the hospital on a rattling gurney, he was shoved in a corner unattended for another hour. He had been hit six times.

A *Los Angeles Times* report indicated that the two bikers unloaded on the unsuspecting undercover agent in the pickup, when in fact only bullets from surrounding police units riddled the truck.

A year later, Harvey was convicted of dual second-degree murder charges and sentenced to two nineteen-year-to-life sentences, although testimony indicated that the undercover officer was not hit with any bullets from Harvey's pistol. A decade later, one of the nineteen-to-life sentences was dropped, but Harvey remains incarcerated as of 2011.

> **Rocky died at the scene and George lay in a pool of blood for more than an hour before he was taken to the hospital.**

As the new decade approached, Terry was forced to face his major demon: drinking. Fortunately he had a knack for building relationships with positive influences. Harry and Alma set him on a path to success. Judge Gately became a lifelong mentor. Harold Tuttle introduced him to motorcycles.

Terry's flair for building positive relationships also helped him sustain them. He was just thirty-three years old and running wild on the streets. His stepfather moved in with him in a small lath-and-plaster duplex on Bruce Street and took over many of his duties as a father.

"Harold and I met at the coffee shop," Terry said. "I was moaning about finding a baby sitter, and he said he could handle it. But he didn't know what he was getting into."

He offered to help with the utility bills. He afforded Terry the opportunity to run even farther amok every night, and he did.

"I had a lot more freedom to run wild," Terry said. "I was drinking every night." Terry's booze of choice was tequila. "Quervo Gold, or Gorilla juice. Made me feel like I was King Kong."

He stayed out to all hours, and often came home so drunk he passed out on the living room floor. One morning behind a terrible hangover, his blustering stepdad confronted him in the hall.

"No more liquor in this house," Harold snapped. "You're no good to your son, no good to anyone while you're drunk. You can sign custody over to me and go be a happy drunk or get over it."

Terry stopped drinking that night and never returned to the bottle. He had enough on his back to drive any man insane. He was left to grapple with the violence, the cops, the politics, the drugs, the back-biting, and the legal battles. He chained-smoked and took up drinking coffee like it was ethyl for his personal Cadillac.

"No more liquor in this house," Harold snapped. "You're no good to your son, no good to anyone while you're drunk. You can sign custody over to me and go be a happy drunk or get over it."

Mexico

DURING THE HOT SUMMER OF 1982, Terry discovered Vago patches being flown in Mexico. Loco and Crazy Johnny, north-of-the-border members, rode into Mexicali to chase whores and discovered a Mexican biker running a makeshift Vago patch. It wasn't a direct copy, just a rough facsimile, but they were using the notorious name. It was unlike any club problem Terry had ever encountered, and it was an ominous one. He wasn't sure what to expect, but it was incumbent upon the Vagos to investigate. As tough as the streets of Los Angeles were, the notion of rolling across the border and facing Mexican charters was daunting.

"We didn't know if we would return," Terry said, so he made sure every brother knew what might lie ahead before they rolled toward

Members of the Tijuana Chapter of the Vagos, outside their clubhouse in 2001. The Vagos established ten Mexican chapters from Tijuana to Mexico City.

During the hot summer of 1982, Terry discovered Vago patches being flown in Mexico.

the border. "Parts put a crew of fifteen-twenty members together for the run."

On a hot summer morning at 6:00, the brothers rolled out of the San Gabriel Valley clubhouse, a long, hidden, clapboard building next to an old Spanish home owned by a silent movie star. It rested on a dirt road overlooking the San Gabriel River bed. They fired up their choppers and rolled through the back streets of Rosemead until they hit the Interstate 10 freeway east into Berdoo. They stopped for gas, then rode to Indio, cutting off the freeway at Highway 86 near La Quinta and the notorious Coachella Valley, heading south along the Salton Sea into Brawley, then into El Centro and Calexico on the north side of the Mexican border at Mexicali.

Centuries earlier the Spanish had arrived in the area after crossing the Sonora Desert's *Camino del Diablo*, or Devil's Road. The Spaniards nearly wiped out the native population, although a few surviving indigenous Cocopah people still lived in a government-protected corner of the delta close to the junction of the Hardy and Colorado rivers. Because of flooding the Spanish and Mexican population had little to do with the northeastern corner of the Baja California peninsula, because they perceived it to be an untamable desert delta.

In the mid-19th century a geologist working for the Southern Pacific Railroad came to the delta area, discovering what the native Yumans had known for centuries: The thick river sediment deposits made the area prime farming land. These sediments extended far to the west of the river itself, accumulating in a shallow basin below the Sierra de Cucapá.

In 1900, the U.S.-based California Development Company received permission from the Díaz government to cut a canal through the delta's Arroyo Alamo, linking the dry basin with the Colorado River. To attract farmers to the area, the developers named it the Imperial Valley. In 1903, the first 500 farmers arrived; by late 1904, 100,000 acres of valley were irrigated, and

10,000 people had settled on the land, harvesting cotton, fruits, and vegetables. The concentration of small housing units that straddled the border was called Calexico on the U.S. side, Mexicali on the Mexican side.

The Vagos approached Mexicali, about 130 miles east of San Diego, The capital of the state of Baja California, Mexicali was the second largest city in Baja with a population of just under 400,000. The Vagos rolled up to the border crossing. Terry was in the lead on his long, green *Lady and the Tramp* Shovelhead chopper, followed by his cadre of green outlaws. The border guards didn't blink and waved the gang of rough-looking bikers through.

Mexicali wasn't as rough as some of the other Mexican border towns, such as Tijuana but the brothers kept their eyes open as they rumbled through the blistering desert town looking for bikers or a connection with the unofficial Vagos club. The brothers found a park across from an old cathedral surrounding a concrete fountain in the center of town, pulled over, and dismounted. A local vendor approached with a pushcart full of sodas. Unfortunately, the Cokes were as hot as the cracked pavement surrounding the fountain. The Vagos popped the pressurized cans seeking relief from the steamy heat, but found none in the boiling soda.

Mexicali wasn't as rough as some of the other Mexican border towns, such as Tijuana, but the brothers kept their eyes open.

While some of the brothers rested under shade trees, Parts, Crazy Johnny, and Prophet decided to continue the hunt down narrow streets without the conspicuous pack following. It wasn't long before Parts discovered a handful of Harleys parked in front of a bar. One of the bikes belonged to a Mexican "Vago," who immediately treated Parts with respect. When Parts asked for a meeting, the member suggested a saloon across from the central park. Parts explained that the IP— Prophet was the international president at that time—was waiting, and the young man's eyes widened like a spot-lighted deer. A meeting time was set and Parts and his crew returned to the park, where the

"There is only one set of Vagos," Parts said staring the interpreter down. "We don't give a fuck how this goes down, but by at the end of the day, there will still only be one set of Vagos."

brothers determined who would attend the meeting and who would stand watch around the perimeter.

Some fifteen Mexican Vagos rolled up to the bar, most on raggedy Harleys, but a few were on Hondas and Suzukis. They were a small-framed group of very poor riders, but they were highly respectful and considerate as they entered the large saloon. Six California Vagos, including Terry, Parts, and Prophet, pulled up chairs at a long western-styled table.

"It was intense," Terry said.

Parts stood as the Mexican cadre of green outlaws with makeshift colors, some handmade, wandered silently into the room. Some sat at the table while others backed apprehensively against the wall and folded their arms or stuffed their hands in their pockets. Parts was always the front-line man.

A Mexican member offered up a Spanish interpreter, and Parts lit into him.

"Why the hell are you flying Vago patches?" he demanded to know.

"We saw them in a magazine," the interpreter returned after requesting an answer from one of his members.

"There is only one set of Vagos," Parts said staring the interpreter down. "We don't give a fuck how this goes down, but by at the end of the day, there will still only be one set of Vagos."

The interpreter wiped his sweating brow with a green bandana and quickly interpreted Parts's words to his brothers.

"We mean no disrespect," the dark young interpreter responded. "We want to be a part of the Vagos and will do whatever it takes."

Parts didn't back up for a second. He told them that they couldn't run makeshift Vago patches, that only one version was approved. The Mexican brothers explained how poor they were, and that they were forced to make whatever patches they could muster.

Parts told them the rules, the Vago code, and the chain of command. As the meeting progressed the tension subsided inside, but the brothers standing watch on the outside in the blistering heat needed to know the score. Terry stepped outside and brought his brothers up to speed.

At that juncture, the Mexican contingent of Vagos had thirty members, and the women wore the same patches as the men. Terry explained the Vago mantra, and that if they planned to run the name the patches had to be approved, and women could not wear the same patch as the brothers.

The meeting proceeded better than Terry ever imagined, and the Mexican brothers took the Northern Vagos to a Chinese restaurant for dinner, then to an all-night strip joint for a party with members of other local clubs, including the Solo Angels. As the sun sent scorching wake-up rays across the river delta, the California brothers mounted their rides and headed north toward home.

> "We mean no disrespect," the dark young interpreter responded. "We want to be a part of the Vagos and will do whatever it takes."

For the next couple of years, the Northern Vagos kept a close eye on the Mexican charter. Loco, one of the young San Bernardino brothers who had discovered the Mexican Vagos, became deathly ill over the next six months and died on an operating table during stomach surgery. If he had lived, he would have seen the Mexican Vagos organization grow into something much different from the rag-tag bunch of bikers he first discovered. They remained a poor lot, riding whatever they could cobble together—life south of the border didn't offer a lot of opportunity to get ahead in life—but the Vagos to the north helped their southern brothers. As northern brothers replaced their worn patches or brothers retired, they sent their used or tattered patches south to help shift the Mexican Vagos from handmade patches to approved, embroidered Vago emblems.

One strong Mexican member, P.C., became close to Terry. They first met at Terry's shop when P.C. rode up to discuss club business.

Terry explained the Vago mantra, and that if they planned to run the name the patches had to be approved, and women could not wear the same patch as the brothers.

P.C. was short, with long, straight dark hair and a penchant for massive silver jewelry, including elaborate engraved silver conchos on long leather wrist gauntlets.

"He had a bitch about a member using heroin," Terry said. "I told him we had a zero-tolerance rule when it came to hard shit."

P.C. became the boss of the Mexicali charter, but he worked in the U.S., built a home, and returned the money he made to his homeland. He turned the Mexicali clubhouse shack into a righteous clubhouse where the bathrooms were clean and club families could live comfortably.

One year during the holidays, Terry rode south to visit P.C. and attended one of their meetings. At one point during the evening gathering in the clubhouse, Terry left the room. When he returned, the brothers had all stepped forward, all fifty of them, and removed their patches and placed them reverently on the pool table before leaving.

"I was shocked," Terry said. "I thought they were giving up their shit."

As it turned out P.C. had organized a toy run through the streets of Mexicali to deliver toys to the poor kids and he wanted to ensure that his brothers got their asses up in time and made the run.

"If any member didn't show up for the event," P.C. said, "they were out."

Every member showed up the next morning to back the effort for the kids of Mexicali. P.C. also supported orphanages, the homeless, and children's hospitals.

"He would make runs to the garment district in Los Angeles," Terry said. "He bought new clothes by the bundle for the kids in Mexico."

As the years passed, ten Vago chapters spread across the country all the way south to Mexico City. It wasn't without its glitches. At one point, a Mexican Vago attempted to rule the Mexican chapters. He pushed brothers around and told them he had a letter from

Terry proclaiming him to be the Mexican I.P. Terry and Freeway Pete, another member, rode to Mexico. Freeway Pete spoke Spanish fluently and could understand every word of bullshit this brother spread. Freeway Pete, a monster of a man, stood quietly to the side and listened to his Mexican counterpart ramble on to his brothers about a written agreement with Terry.

"He buried himself right in front of us," Terry said. His lies were revealed and his patch was pulled.

Another time, Terry rode with P.C. out of Mexicali, south to San Felipe for a President's Day party. There was a long, straight stretch of highway, more than 100 miles over open terrain.

"We got on that hot-as-hell highway and started to fly along at over 100 mph," Terry said. "We were cooking when I started to hear hollering."

> Freeway Pete, a monster of a man, stood quietly to the side and listened to his Mexican counterpart ramble on to his brothers about a written agreement with Terry.

Over the roar of the Harleys and the 100-mph wind whistling past Terry's ears, P.C. screamed, "Alto, Alto!"

In the distance he could see something, a blip on the horizon. It was a Federale roadblock. Terry slammed on his rear brake (he had no front brake, just a spool hub) and started to skid over the slick, smoldering asphalt toward the roadblock.

As he entered the government checkpoint, automatic weapons were cocked and readied. Terry skidded right past the checkpoint before bringing his long chopper to a stop. P.C. pulled into the checkpoint and immediately negotiated with the pissed-off officers. The Federales were stopping any passing motorists and working them over for money or even cold drinks.

"Alto means to stop," P.C. told Terry as they rolled away from the checkpoint and kept the speed down for the last half of the trip onto the beach in San Felipe.

It was smoldering hot as they rumbled into the coastal town where the Sea of Cortez, the Baja desert, and 10,000-foot mountains come together, and onto the soft sand beach. Terry couldn't take it for another minute. He scrambled off his bike and ran for the water's edge and the soft rolling surf. Unfortunately, the salty brine was as hot as warm bath water and not the refreshing splash of moisture he sought.

The party started and the brothers drank warm beers, smoked the finest Mexican cannabis, and howled at the moon into the night. At 2:00 in the morning, Terry felt something jab him in the ribs. It was the barrel of a gun.

He scrambled out of the tent he shared with Carrie, a petite blonde from Southern California who rode her own trike. The area was surrounded by Federales searching for bottles or any sign of drinking. Once more, P.C. negotiated with the military horde armed with automatic weapons.

> ## At 2:00 in the morning, Terry felt something jab him in the ribs. It was the barrel of a gun.

"We were scared to death," Terry said. "I don't like the uncertainty."

The rule called for no drinking on President's Day, anywhere. All the brothers were pulled from their tents and searched.

The next morning they rolled north from San Felipe toward Mexicali. The little five-foot tall blonde from Hacienda Heights held fast to his tall chromed sissybar. Carrie, with her perky tits and tight pants, was just another hot outlaw groupie looking for sinister times with madmen on motorcycles, and she hooked up with the boss. Her long, straight, southern California blonde hair was pulled tight into a ponytail. She was cute, but she was trouble and had twin boys.

On the outskirts of San Felipe, they pulled over for a taco-and-cerveza breakfast before hitting the long road to Mexicali. Terry bought Carrie a couple of tacos, which she devoured and asked for more. Terry obliged, and then noticed a bevy of young puppy dogs roaming through the makeshift lean-to shack.

The girl immediately fell in love with the soft, multi-colored mutts scampering around the shack.

"Would you like a puppy?" Terry asked

"Yes, but we can't take one home," she responded.

"Oh, you're taking one home," Terry said pointing at her steaming tacos.

"She threw up everywhere," Terry said. ☠

Cold-Blooded Hawthorne Attack

THE VAGOS BUILT A MENACING REPUTATION throughout the southland as wild bastards who had no concern for the law, their community, or even other bikers; they only cared about protecting club members.

Terry and Parts recognized their responsibility for the growing harassment from authorities. In this the Vagos weren't alone; other clubs earned equally nefarious reputations as unruly menaces on the streets and likewise had to deal with vast numbers of their memberships being jailed. Law enforcement rapidly turned against all bikers, resulting in an atmosphere not unlike the belligerent feuds that destroyed entire communities in the hinterlands of Appalachia—not surprising, given that many of the men who started the motorcycle clubs of Southern California were Okies, descendants of a long line of people who emigrated westward across the continent

Terry the Wall leaning on a Harley-Davidson Knucklehead chopper being built in an apartment living room. Still smiling, he is now six feet, six inches and weighs over 300 pounds, a monster.

Not all members were pleased with the public's perception of club members as out-of-control Berserkers hell-bent on destroying everything in their paths.

until they finally ran into the Pacific Ocean and were forced to stop.

Not all members were pleased with the public's perception of club members as out-of-control Berserkers hell-bent on destroying everything in their paths. Some bikers and clubs, such as Terry and the Vagos, sought to alter or even soften the negative attitude toward bikers by organizing toy runs, charity efforts, and blood drives.

In May of 1983, 30 Vagos led by a highly-educated member named Rat rolled into the Orange County Red Cross station in an effort to give blood, as a token gesture to the community and specifically to law enforcement. They intended to prove the Vagos were more than a purely criminal organization.

Rat came to the Vagos after he studied outlaw motorcycle clubs at Florida State University during a class on social anthropology. He became fascinated with club life.

"I was drawn to this group," Rat said. " I realized almost right away that I didn't want to study this way of life; I wanted to live it. It was the only example that I can think of in which this society allows us to choose our own family, and that's what a club is: a family."

"Rat was a brilliant nut," Terry said. "He was able to speak twenty different languages."

Rat was a six-foot-tall, balding, scroungy bastard. He had a poodle that he jacked off in front of brothers.

"You never drank out of a bottle after he did," Terry said.

One time he staggered into a campfire, drunk and swinging a sword. One of the other members, Willy, shouted, "It's Rat, the sword swallower."

Rat spun, lifted his shaggy head, and swallowed the sword. He was a member of the Vagos for fifteen years.

Rat and Wolfman, the chapter president, led the pack of Vagos into the Red Cross facility, where they gave blood and luckily drew coverage in the *LA Times* for their good deed. After the blood drive they rode into Trabuco Canyon, in the Orange County foothills, for a keg party, offsetting their good behavior with 120 gallons of beer.

Vagos lived at the junction of the tracks between good and evil. Even within the ranks, brothers fought brothers over the notion of brotherhood, like any family organization, a mixture of structure and benevolence. It was a life that pitted the outlaw's warrior spirit against the evil ranks of criminal minds. Sometimes the noble outlaw spirit and the evil criminal mind occupied the same flesh-and-blood vessel. This inner contradiction manifested itself in outward actions. There boiled a growing competition between clubs to determine which was the baddest, most evil criminal organization. It was a seriously destructive competition that could only lead to boastful chest-pounding while behind bars.

> After the blood drive they rode into Trabuco Canyon, in the Orange County foothills, for a keg party, offsetting their good behavior with 120 gallons of beer.

The authorities, and even some within the Vagos ranks, saw charity work as a bullshit sign of weakness. You're either an outlaw or you're not, they argued, but the community, religious groups, sensible members, and family members hoped and prayed for a higher aspiration, a compassionate, organized group of brothers with a positive purpose.

Suddenly, in September of 1983, the Vagos club's mettle was tested at a much higher level, and again they tasted wrongdoing by the law. In July of the same year, a young Vago named Ray Malloy was jumped in the Country Girl Bar in Hawthorne, California. Three locals with knives rat-packed Malloy and stabbed him several times. Malloy managed to roll free of his attackers on the dirty country-western barroom floor, pull his own blade, and jump back into the fray. He escaped after inflicting several wounds on his assailants.

Three locals with knives rat-packed Malloy and stabbed him several times.

The Hawthorne cops were summoned and reports taken. At first the cops were keen on hunting the three knife-wielding attackers, until they discovered that the victim was a member of the Vagos. A hunt was launched for Malloy and charges filed against the biker. The Hawthorne police, with combined agencies and a local judge, filed for twenty legitimate search warrants and twenty-three illegitimate warrants, raiding forty-three homes in six weeks. They stormed Vagos's residences, relatives' houses, and known and suspected associates' living quarters, anyone who might be harboring Malloy.

Cops bludgeoned front doors from Hawthorne to Apple Valley, and even dragged a pregnant woman awaiting a Caesarean section into the street. They yanked a handicapped girl out of bed. A licensed child-care operator tending to five babies was tossed into her front yard. The police were heavily armed as they kicked down doors, suspecting retaliation from armed Vagos. No retaliation came as they dragged naked senior citizens from their homes into their front yards.

By September they still had not found their man. Residents of fifteen of the invaded homes had absolutely no affiliation to the Vagos. Petrified by the attack, only one family filed a formal complaint. Some homes belonged to ex-members of the Vagos who had left the club years ago. Homeowners who testified to no connection with the club still had property confiscated. Court records documented seizure of guns, mail, cash, bills, motorcycles, photo albums, and a Porsche.

"I have never heard of the Vagos," said a Lawndale woman. She was the licensed child-care operator who was baby-sitting five small children when her home was invaded by six armed plainclothes police officers. "I never heard of this man, Ruby Red, who they said they were looking for. I couldn't believe it. I don't feel safe here anymore."

Hawthorne Officer Frazier developed the attack list from a roster he seized from a Vagos member's home. The member, Richard (Blue) Beaulieu, was later shown the document by a reporter.

"Hey, that's my writing," Blue said. "I wrote that more than two years ago when the South Bay chapter was just starting."

How could a sophisticated law enforcement agency stoop so low? Roger Ely, a plumbing contractor, heard thumping outside his home, like men marching. Then he heard rounds being jacked into the chambers of shotguns, so he opened his front door. He was handcuffed, searched, and questioned. It wasn't until one of the officers recognized him as the brother of a Torrance police officer that they quit searching and destroying his premises. Cops had become the outlaws they were searching for, and they thought their mismanagement was, in a word, "funny."

In a sense, they were far worse than the stand-up Vagos they were chasing. Most Vagos were noted outlaws but they proudly admitted it. They wore a patch proclaiming their affiliation. They didn't hide behind a badge, an undercover police car, or use a judge and the legal system to clean up the messes left by their misdeeds.

> **Cops had become the outlaws they were searching for, and they thought their mismanagement was, in a word, "funny."**

Terry had moved to Cherry Lee and managed seven lath-and-plaster bungalows. The Hawthorne police stormed all seven units. One cottage was the home of the pregnant woman mentioned above.

Another woman, Sandy Johnston, who was frisked in her front yard, said, "I had nothing to do with them (Vagos), and should have known that before they came barging in. If they have a reason for it, I'm all for it, but they didn't. I don't take drugs. I don't like drugs. I don't even like beer. I don't even smoke cigarettes!"

The cops also raided the cottage occupied by her mother and mentally handicapped sister; neither had any connection to the Vagos.

A number listed as belonging to Bruce (Panhead) Cooper, actually belonged to a Torrance housewife.

"I was stark naked getting into the shower," she said, when a half-dozen armed police started to kick in her door. While she fumbled

"It's your word
against ours,"
a Hawthorne
cop told her,
"unless your dog
decides to talk."

for a bathrobe, a Hawthorne police officer shot her. She was dragged from her residence and thrown in her front yard. They searched her drawers and closets, finally taking bank statements and a photograph of her husband.

"We couldn't understand why," the unidentified woman said. "We're average Joe Blow citizens. No record. No drugs. No reason anything like this should happen."

What was her connection to Panhead Cooper? She was a part-time baby sitter and he was a customer from time to time. He moved away eighteen months prior and she never heard from him again. She tried to file a complaint with the Hawthorne police, but she wasn't hopeful.

"It's your word against ours," a Hawthorne cop told her, "unless your dog decides to talk."

The cop behind the illicit raids said his intelligence-gathering procedure to establish probable cause for the warrants was, "really good, but not perfect." He stated that he depended on tips from officers in other agencies who were gang specialists, and he admitted that he was not an expert.

When the shit hit the fan publicly in the *Los Angeles Times*, various agencies tried to separate themselves from the Hawthorne unit. Claire Spiegel reported that officers for the LA Sheriff's Department were not pleased with the manner in which Frazier handled supplied information. It was a mess.

It was 6:30 in the morning when a cluster of armed, plainclothes cops in flak jackets surrounded Terry's bungalow. Terry stepped suspiciously onto the porch to investigate his barking dogs, only to be charged by the dark, unmarked officers. He stepped quickly back inside, but they stormed his flat, smacked him in the face with a shotgun butt, and they stuck a shotgun in the face of his fourteen-year-old son, then dragged him outside. They ransacked his home. What they didn't take, they smashed. Terry had a collection of crystal bells neatly positioned on polished wooden shelves in his living room. One officer smacked them one at a time with his billy club.

"Are you going to talk?" the officer asked as he destroyed Terry's collection. The Hawthorne unit dragged Terry into his front yard and beat him with billy clubs and batons.

"They would have beat me to death if the El Monte cops didn't show up," Terry said.

The authorities' actions went against the code of the West, or in keeping with the nature of the outlaw versus the Man. If a club member was busted or raided, he was generally left to his own devices to survive and retrieve any confiscated materials. If a cop grabbed an outlaw's shit, usually he could keep whatever he wanted as long as he dropped whatever trumped-up charges he dreamed up. For the brothers to stand up to the cops, they had to risk losing everything, plus the threat of increased prosecution and harassment. The Man could make life mighty rough on unsophisticated outlaws.

As soon as he was released, Terry and Parts scrambled across town to meet with Parts's former attorney, Joanne Bockian.

"We needed to get our bikes back pronto," Terry said. But they also proposed a civil suit.

But the case rapidly grew from recovering several confiscated motorcycles to dealing with forty-seven illegal break-ins, which involved more than 300 cops from a dozen Los Angeles municipalities. At one point they dragged the seventy-one-year-old father of an ex-Vago out of his bathroom and held him naked on his couch. A frightened toddler was smacked with the butt of a shotgun. Few of the victims had any connection to the Vagos. According to the warrants, sheriff's deputies were searching for Malloy, his knife, and his bloody T-shirt. But they helped themselves to anything.

> It was 6:30 in the morning when a cluster of armed, plainclothes cops in flak jackets surrounded Terry's bungalow.

"What the cops didn't haul away, they destroyed," Terry said.

The massive conflict was on between the stand-up "evil" bikers and the utterly corrupt Hawthorne city police operation.

Harassment escalated. The entire Vago organization was under fire. Finally, two months later, in November, 1983, under extreme pressure Ray Charles Malloy, forty-three, a member of the South Bay Chapter of the Vagos, surrendered himself and entered the Los Angeles County Jail. After attacking the southland, searching forty-seven residences, destroying or confiscating personal property, documents, and vehicles, and questioning hundreds of supposed Vago affiliates, the authorities from a dozen agencies could not find Malloy.

The *LA Times* reported Malloy wanted three Hispanics to speak English at the Hawthorne bar, so they jumped him and stabbed him, but he fought back. Malloy continued to ride to work every day, but the pressure on the club rubbed off on him and he decided enough was enough, plus he was uncomfortable being on the run, although he never left town. Still the all-powerful Man couldn't find him. The irony was overwhelming.

Terry, the president of the San Gabriel Chapter and national vice president by that time, along with Parts, added up the claims, the attacks on innocent folks, the missing property, and decided to jam their Vago transmission into overdrive and sue the Man. This would mean additional harassment and loss of any confiscated property. The chances of winning, for any outlaw organization, were one hundred to one. Terry reached out to the American Civil Liberties Union (ACLU).

The chances of winning, for any outlaw organization, were one hundred to one.

In most cases, especially for motorcycle clubs, help would not be forthcoming, but Paul Hoffman, a middle-aged ACLU attorney with a beer belly, offered organizational assistance. Joanne Bockian, Parts's cute little attorney, also jumped into the fray and in April of 1984 she accused the Hawthorne cops of assault and battery, infliction of emotional distress, unconstitutional invasion of privacy, unlawful search and seizure, false arrest, and use of excessive force during the raids in Hawthorne and fourteen other communities.

The only crime claimed by the authorities was association with the Vagos Motorcycle Club. Bockian and the ACLU filed a $9-million suit against the police for the tactics they used during the manhunt. The officers exceeded the limits of their court-ordered documents in forty-seven warrants, some illegally procured, when they roughed up residents and seized property not mentioned in the court orders. Bockian called it, "using force and tactics designed to instill fear . . . which was unnecessary, unreasonable, and unwarranted."

The lawsuit claimed police broke down doors without trying to gain peaceful entry, displayed guns and batons "in a rude and threatening manner," failed to identify themselves properly, herded naked or partially clad residents before other police or neighbors, and handcuffed residents and forced them to lie face-down in their front yards for hours while they searched and destroyed their homes.

Hawthorne police refused to return seized property of the seventy-eight residents or even to provide them with claim forms. The suit sought $15,000 for each plaintiff, for emotional anguish, humiliation, and shock, plus $100,000 in punitive damages. The document called the attack, "flagrant harassment."

In 1986, in the midst of the Hawthorne case, Terry was elected the club's international president. With his stepbrother at his side, Terry would lead the Vagos into the ACLU-supported legal battle in the Man's courtrooms and on the Man's terms. This would be a legal first in the annals of outlaw motorcycle club history.

Suddenly the shoe was on the other foot after twenty years of police harassment. Terry and Parts, with the Vagos behind them, were prepared to dig in for the long haul. They knew the city of Hawthorne would attempt every legal maneuver known in order to grind the legal wheels to a halt and pile on the financial cost of the case to break the club down.

With his stepbrother at his side, Terry would lead the Vagos into the ACLU-supported legal battle in the Man's courtrooms and on the Man's terms.

The Gestapo tactics unleashed by the Hawthorne Police on the Vagos didn't let up, nor were they limited to the Vagos.

Immediately Hawthorne PD attorneys initiated delay tactics.

The night after the lawsuit was filed, Joanne snatched the opportunity to become a plaintiff. Joanne, Terry, Parts, and a couple of other members visited the Hawthorne PD headquarters to retrieve their confiscated motorcycles and guns.

"I had never been to Hawthorne," Terry said. "We arrived at 5:00 p.m. with all the appropriate documents, but the Hawthorne Police refused to turn over our property." Joanne argued with the duty officer, called the chief of police, the mayor, and finally a judge. "It said 'forthwith' on the documents, which means 'right now.' "

"They didn't turn over our property until 1:00 in the morning," Terry said, "then they gave us a police escort to the freeway."

After that night the short, ambitious Joanne added herself to the case hoping to collect damages in addition to her fees. Her scandalous behavior didn't end in the Hawthorne PD waiting room.

The Gestapo tactics unleashed by the Hawthorne Police on the Vagos didn't let up, nor were they limited to the Vagos. In November the Los Angeles County grand jury indicted a female Hawthorne police officer for kicking an unconscious, handcuffed prisoner. Brutality complaints ran rampant in the South Bay department. Just a couple months earlier a Sherman Oaks attorney, George Denny III, served the Hawthorne agency with a civil complaint on behalf of seven people who claimed to be beaten and falsely arrested by Hawthorne cops in January of 1983.

Denny accused the department of an "ongoing conspiracy" to manhandle prisoners. It was a time of rampant excessive force in the crowded, seaside party community. The criminal edict originated from the top of the heap, in this case the chief, Kenneth Stonebraker, who smirked in the *Los Angeles Times*, "The complaints are from that faction who does wrong things. They don't like an active department."

Beginning in 1982, claims against the Hawthorne department for false arrest and misconduct escalated. In 1983, eighty-three complaints were filed, including the thirty-three from the Vagos' bust. Stonebraker felt that the ends justified the means. "Since 1980, we've reduced crime and doubled our arrests," he told the *Los Angeles Times*.

Stonebraker felt that the ends justified the means. "Since 1980, we've reduced crime and doubled our arrests," he told the *Los Angeles Times*.

In many ways the police were not unlike the motorcycle clubs they harassed. Like clubs pushing their weight around against other clubs or locals, police departments can behave in much the same way when they suffer from poor, egotistical police leadership. Under such circumstances the police are as likely to stray beyond legal boundaries as the members of outlaw clubs.

The police problem wasn't just in Hawthorne. Within a fifteen-mile radius along the west coast of Los Angeles, twenty isolated communities shared the same freeways and main concrete arteries. Incorporated in 1922, the City of Hawthorne currently has a population of nearly 87,000 within a six square mile area. It's located near the Los Angeles International Airport, connected by rail to the Port of Los Angeles and downtown Los Angeles, and surrounded by the San Diego (I-405), Harbor (I-110), and Glenn M. Anderson (I-105) Freeways. Because of its location, Hawthorne could call itself the "Hub of the South Bay," although its real claim to fame was as the birthplace of the pop group The Beach Boys. It is virtually surrounded by eight Los Angeles suburbs: Lennox, Del Air, Lawndale, West Athens, Inglewood, Gardena, Westmont, and Alondra Park. They are all teeming asphalt and stucco jungles crammed next to one another. There is no open space, unless a Vago rides his motorcycle across the sandy beach into the Pacific. A rider would be forced to travel 100 miles inland to the Mojave Desert or the San Bernardino mountains to escape the urban squalor.

Officers who
weren't on
board with
Hawthorne's
storm trooper
methods were
transferred,
given
involuntary
retirement, or
threatened with
being kicked out.

This was the fiefdom over which Chief Stonebraker presided. Stonebraker was as much an outlaw as any member of the Vagos. He grew up in Hawthorne and spent most of his life and his entire career working as a cop there. He took over the department in 1981, and all hell broke lose. Stonebraker felt it was time to make a name for himself. He either initiated the bad-boy attitude among the local officers or he couldn't control the bullies on his force. Either way, his ascension meant that Hawthorne became a lawless town.

Officers who weren't on board with Hawthorne's storm trooper methods were transferred, given involuntary retirement, or threatened with being kicked out. "Several officers and officials would talk about the department only if they were not identified," wrote *Times* staff writer Gerald Faris in his article on Stonebraker.

"There was no training, no procedures, no manual," Faris quoted the city clerk Patrick Keller, saying as he recalled a reserve officer briefing. "They just told us, 'Okay boys, go out and get 'em.'"

"You learned from the best officers, or the worst," said another city employee.

Terry and the Vagos had their hands full.

For seven long years, the battle raged on between the ACLU and the Vagos motorcycle club and the Hawthorne cops. Terry and Parts put up the initial legal funding and received some help from the ACLU, which was then under the leadership of Paul Hoffman. Hoffman litigated more than twenty civil rights/civil liberties cases between 1976 and 1984, specializing in cases involving First Amendment rights, criminal law and procedure, freedom of information and privacy, and police misconduct, which meant the Vagos's case was right up his alley. Hoffman researched every element in the Vagos's case; he questioned each witness, studied each damaged home, documented every missing piece of property, and collected depositions from every plaintiff, including Terry's son, Boomer, who was fourteen at the time of the break-in.

"Three cops stormed my bedroom, like special forces attacking an enemy enclave," Terry Jr. said. "They all had weapons drawn and were screaming, 'Get up! Don't move! Get up! Don't move!' I sat up and asked 'em, 'What's it going to be, get up or don't move?' " Rather than answering Boomer's sensible question, they pointed a shotgun at the fourteen-year-old's face.

"I never understood the attack on all the residents around us," Boomer said. "They were all just citizens. They had nothing to do with bikers or clubs."

Boomer, who was starting to go by the name "Terry the Wall," grew from fourteen to twenty-one years of age during this conflict with the Hawthorne PD. At twenty-one, he was six-feet, six-inches tall and weighed more than 300 pounds—hence the name "Terry the Wall." When he got old enough he started to work as a security guard for rock tours and at the Whiskey A Go-Go, Roxy, and Rainbow night clubs in Hollywood.

Ten causes for action were filed in a thirty-page legal brief, listing plaintiffs from sixteen municipalities. While the Hawthorne legal team ground the case to a halt in court, the Vagos faced escalated harassment and more unjustified arrests. Their bikes were impounded, and their kids were harassed while walking to and from school. The cops even tried threatening phone calls in the middle of the night to scare off plaintiffs. "We're going to kill you, asshole," an untraceable voice would say over the phone. Even in the face of outright criminal threats from law enforcement, the Vagos didn't give in. The brothers sold motorcycles and organized garage sales and fund-raisers to keep the legal fight alive.

> The cops even tried threatening phone calls in the middle of the night to scare off plaintiffs. "We're going to kill you, asshole," an untraceable voice would say over the phone.

The seventy-one-year-old gentleman who was pulled from his home naked died before the case was aired in court. Several of the original plaintiffs were harassed so severely that they backed out of the suit. Hawthorne faced financial woes, but their best tactic was dragging their feet in an attempt to bankrupt the Vagos and bring their legal battle to an untimely close. The Hawthorne authorities gambled, prolonging the motions and pouring more funds into building their case.

Finally in February of 1990, six years after the original complaint, the case made it to the Los Angeles Superior Court docket. The ACLU and the Vagos were reasonably confident. They had proof of falsified warrants that supported their allegations that every police action was illegal and unjustifiable. There were lengthy complaints and evidence of gross violations of civil rights, excessive force, and damage to personal property. Unfortunately, positioning the Vagos members' statements against the testimony of experienced and knowledgeable professionals put the outlaws in a weak position. Would the jury believe the scruffy outlaws over polished police officers?

"The ACLU team coached us before the trial," Terry the Wall said.

It was a cold, dark, eerie morning outside the massive concrete and marble Los Angeles Superior Court building when the case finally came to trial. The slick, highly paid attorneys for Hawthorne described the Vagos as society's animals, with lengthy criminal records. They documented their arrests and numerous investigations. They were nothing more than drug-using rapists who deserved torture more than simple prosecution. Their violent history earned them nothing more than contempt and banishment.

The case dragged on for almost two months, after almost seven years of abject harassment, rocking back and forth, tipping toward the establishment, then back in favor of the rough-looking bikers. Then one clear, sparkling southern California day, the sun shinned on the Vagos' evil green patch.

Two ex-Hawthorne Police Department members, Dave Griffith and Don Jackson, took the stand on behalf of the defense. They were two honest cops who were swept into a department rampant with corruption as young recruits. They testified to overzealous department policies, illegal practices, excessive force, and falsified records. They even admitted to stealing personal property during raids.

The courtroom testimony suddenly shined a cleansing light on the green club patch and the abused families swept into a case involving outlaw motorcyclists they didn't even know. Attorneys for the city scrambled for a quick cleansing of the open, legal wound. Terry's son was called as the last witness, and the attorneys grilled the fourteen-year-old kid.

"They kept asking the same question over and over," Terry Jr. said. "The judge stood for the first time during the case and hollered back at the district attorney: 'That's enough. He answered honestly the first time.'"

"They kept asking the same question over and over," Terry Jr. said. "The judge stood for the first time during the case and hollered back at the district attorney: 'That's enough. He answered honestly the first time.'"

The case rapidly unraveled right in front of the slick Hawthorne suits. They offered a quick, out-of-court, $1.95 million settlement. Publicity quickly turned against the city, their officials, the police chief, and the legal team. They wanted out, quick. They wanted to patch the hole in the dike and run for higher ground.

"The Hawthorne police were depending on the fact that juries usually believed policemen," Patty Erickson, one of the ACLU attorneys said, "but the Vagos's case proved that juries will believe bikers. Other clubs should not be reluctant to file a civil rights suit. They needn't believe they have to tolerate abuse, or that the decision will always go against them just because they are bikers."

"The raids weren't the worst of it," Parts said. "The raids were just the thing they got caught with."

"If we hadn't stuck it out," Terry said, "they would have gotten away with trampling the law again."

The club was tired of the citywide feud and how it rubbed off on all the cop shops in the surrounding eighty-eight cities, including the infamous Los Angeles City Police Department and the Los Angeles Sheriff's Department. That was a lot of cops roaming over 4,000 square miles of Los Angeles County, with some 10,000 Los Angeles police officers and almost 20,000 Los Angeles County Sheriff deputies against a couple of hundred loosely knit Vagos. The odds were stacked against the green crew.

The Vagos decided to accept the settlement offer, although half of the bounty, if they were able to collect it, would go directly to the legal team. That left less than one million to be split between the remaining seventy defendants, for a take-home amount of $21,000 apiece. The city was in financial trouble and their insurance department was bankrupt.

On the other hand, for the first time in history, a motorcycle club stood up to the Man and was victorious. "I never rode to Hawthorne again," Terry said. "The hottest women in that town couldn't lure me into that shithole."

"I don't think anybody expected a motorcycle club to achieve this kind of victory," said the ACLU's Paul Hoffman, the lead attorney in the case. "But we demonstrated that when anyone's rights are violated, you can get full vindication in our system."

Representatives of the city of Hawthorne had nothing to say outside the courtroom.

"The city was broke," Terry said.

Terry was the last witness to be called, and ultimately did not have to testify on the witness stand.

> "I never rode to Hawthorne again," Terry said. "The hottest women in that town couldn't lure me into that shithole."

"Everything I told them was corroborated by the other witnesses, many of whom were my tenants. It's too bad that the case took so long."

Hoffman hoped the healthy settlement would send a sharp message to the Hawthorne PD to change their abusive tactics.

"The money doesn't matter," said plaintiff Ron Bethal, forty-two. He was yanked from one of Terry's bungalows with his wife, naked, and forced to lie face-down in the grass for more than two hours. "All we wanted was for (police) to get the message that we're people, too, and the law applies to everybody." But would the Vagos ultimately collect the small payment the court afforded them, after seven years and nearly 50 percent swept away to pay legal fees? ☠

The Tramp Becomes the
International President

IT WAS A DOWN TIME FOR MANY CLUBS as the annual Black Hills Rally in Sturgis, South Dakota, came to a close in 1986. It was just the second year after Harley-Davidson introduced the Evolution engine to the market, and low-income club guys didn't yet have access to the more reliable model that would change club life forever. What's more, many bikers had lost faith in the factory. Most one-percenter clubs required their members to ride American-made motorcycles, which meant they had to ride Harley-Davidsons.

That hadn't been much of a hardship in the years before Terry joined the Vagos; up until the mid-1960s Harley-Davidson set the world's standard for big-displacement motorcycles. Then they started to face serious competition, first from Great Britain, then from Japan. By the early 1970s the competition surpassed Harley-Davidson.

Meanwhile Harley continued to fall behind. While the Japanese produced ever larger and better motorcycles, Harley built outdated motorcycles using old technologically, and they suffered from

A young member, Sleeper, standing at the opening to his garage in 1998. He was a kickboxing world champion and member of the Pasadena chapter. He has since retired from the Vagos.

Harley built outdated motorcycles using old technology.

horrendous quality-control issues. By the mid-1970s you were as likely to see a Harley broken down on the side of the road as you were to see one being ridden.

For a while diehards continued to buy Harleys out of sheer force of habit, but eventually customers had their fill of the genuinely lousy motorcycles and quit buying them. The Japanese took over the motorcycle market, driving the British motorcycle industry, which relied on similar antiquated technology and had horrendous quality-control problems of its own, out of business entirely and almost drove Harley out of business.

AMF recognized Harley's problems and kept funding the company during tough times. They even invested in the new Evolution engine, designed in conjunction with Porsche engineers. AMF recognized their lack of motorcycle marketing experience and wanted out, but supported Harley until a new deal was developed. Eventually an investment group put together by several Harley employees took the company off of AMF's hands.

Times were hard at first—Harley's reputation was in the toilet and it was selling a product that represented the technological state-of-the-art circa 1936. The newly independent Harley-Davidson Motor Co. almost went bankrupt several times, but for 1984 the company introduced a new engine that was infinitely more reliable than the antiquated Shovelhead it replaced. To own a Shovelhead was to tell the world that you could overhaul your engine by the side of the road in the middle of the night with nothing more than an adjustable wrench and a Zippo lighter, because sooner or later you would be doing just that. The new engine, called the Evolution, opened up Harley ownership to anyone with a pulse—just sign the papers and start making those monthly payments.

The new engine was a hit among both the public and the enthusiast press, but Harley was in such a deep hole that the success of the Evo, as it came to be known, did not guarantee the company would survive. But after struggling along for a few more years, Harley hit pay dirt. As the 1980s wound down, the Harley-Davidson motorcycle, with its reliable Evo engine, became the ultimate accessory for celebrities. Many of the stars who began riding Harleys could barely fill their own gas tanks, much less rebuild a V-twin engine, but with the new Evo that was skill enough to gain membership into the brotherhood of Harley-Davidson. As more and more celebrities began appearing in public aboard Harley-Davidson motorcycles, the bikes became the must-have status symbol for the yuppies of the period and sales skyrocketed. This allowed president Vaughn Beals and the company the financial freedom to run Harley-Davidson without interference from bankers. They actually had cash on hand for the first time in a decade.

The mid-1980s was a period of transition for many clubs across the nation. They had fought the wars and struggled with their choppers for decades, but it was all about to change, and it was a time to step up or be stepped on.

All this happened during a time when the rest of the motorcycle industry was still trying to recover from the recession of the early 1980s. Overall, motorcycle sales were plummeting. During this continuing motorcycle sales decline, Harley-Davidson was the only motorcycle company in the world to witness increased sales. Eventually they overtook Honda's market share in the large-displacement motorcycle category.

The reliability of the new Evolution big twin changed the biker lifestyle for the better, at least when it came to the quality of American motorcycles, but in other ways the situation was becoming far more difficult. Police harassment was at an all-time high, and club membership faltered. The Vagos Motorcycle Club was no exception. The mid-1980s was a period of transition for many clubs across the nation. They had fought the wars and struggled with their choppers for decades, but it was all about to change, and it was a time to step up or be stepped on.

Terry was one of those rare individuals who sensed tension in his own ranks and responded. Vago charters grew thin. Lots of brothers were sequestered in the joint or sitting at home in front of television sets and not riding. Terry was the president of the San Gabriel Valley chapter at the end of September 1986, when his brother Parts called.

"I'm going to retire if we don't do something," he said, and hung up.

The annual officers' meeting would be hosted by the Desert Hot Springs chapter. The Hot Springs green gang snatched a plot of desert land at the base of the little San Bernardino Mountains and lined up a series of ratty motor homes in a circle, like covered wagons, surrounding their bonfire pit. A month before the meeting, Terry rode out with a handful of brothers and a massive Vago named Lurch, who was just out of the joint, and built like Hulk Hogan.

"The farther we rolled away from town, the more nervous Lurch became," Terry said. "When we rolled off the highway, he started to look for an escape route." The more rural the area in which the brothers rode, the more tension filled the hot desert air.

"Lurch was sweating bullets," Terry said, "when we rolled up to these crappy motor homes in middle of nowhere."

Lurch thought for sure someone in the joint had ratted him out for speaking to the wrong clique of gangsters in the joint. It wasn't until big Butch, a jailhouse brother, stepped out of one of the motor homes that the tension subsided.

"It was finally like old home week," Terry said. "The brother had nothing to worry about."

As September rolled toward a close, Terry, Sonny, and Jerry the Jew rode their choppers once more toward the grubby side of the desert on the north side of Interstate 10, opposite slick, upscale Palm Springs. They rode off the highway, away from the city, away from any civilization, deep into the desert where no one wanted to be for any length of time, especially in September's blistering heat.

They pulled up to the circled tin wagons and met all the officers of their charters in the center near the fire pit. There was tension in the air as Terry confronted the three-year international president of the Vagos, Leonard Berella.

"There was no vote," Terry said. "I told Jerry the Jew, if he runs at me, I'm going to kill him."

Leonard, wearing leathers, stood fuming in the blistering heat surrounded by his small supporting group of members. He was just five-feet, five-inches tall, but weighed close to 300 pounds. Although he was obese, his thin beard was closely cropped, and his long, stringy black hair was tied neatly at the back of his neck. He confronted Terry, but his support group faltered, and Terry held fast. He knew some of his poor decisions were the cause of the faltering Vagos membership. Terry stepped up and was supported by the chapter leadership. Leonard left the meeting and the Vagos that afternoon.

"He fucked up big time," Terry said, but he gave Leonard the opportunity to leave the club with his patch as a full member. "He was a good dude, just not a leader."

When the brothers rode out of the desert sand in September of 1986, they headed down a new green road. "We would be more active and more involved," Terry said. "We started to help the homeless in our community and run blood drives."

One of Terry's first moves included reaching out to other clubs to resolve conflicts. "Many of the old traditional clubs faced the same obstacles we faced," Terry said. "They were faltering, and some of the big clubs saw it as an opportunity to pounce, but I didn't see it that way." He stood up for some of the small historic clubs. "We needed to keep them alive."

He ruled with an iron fist, appointing his staff without a vote.

"I needed to work with people who could work with me," Terry said. "I was told in the early years that if I was boss, I wasn't in the position to make everyone happy. I needed to develop a strong, functioning organization that works for the whole."

And so his rule began. 🏴‍☠️

> "There was no vote," Terry said. "I told Jerry the Jew, if he runs at me, I'm going to kill him."

Triple T Choppers

TRIPLE T CHOPPERS WAS TERRY'S HOME away from home from 1988 until 2002. It was a place where Terry could hang out and find relief. Triple T stood for Terry, Tekla, and Terry Jr. Although Terry and Tekla hadn't made a very good romantic couple, they made excellent friends and Tekla remains an important part of Terry's life to this day, so much so that she became the middle "T" in "Triple T Choppers."

"I always dreamed of owning a shop," Terry said. "Plus I could keep club action away from my home. We had a meeting place."

It rapidly became a gathering place for anyone who was interested in custom bikes and the lifestyle. Even a local LA Sheriff's deputy stopped twice a week and delivered coffee and donuts.

"He was close to retiring," Terry said of the short, balding deputy. "He never asked about the club; he just talked motorcycles."

Triple T Choppers, shown on the day it was raided in 2006, was Terry's sanctuary for building motorcycles for over a decade, a meeting place for club guys, and sometimes a home for wayward brothers.

On alternate days a railroad union worker wandered into the strip-mall shop, sandwiched between a head shop, a pet shop, a rehab center for recovering addicts, a baseball card shop, and Andy's liquor store on the corner. He delivered the morning supply of pastries and steaming cups of java.

One shiny southern California morning, as Terry arrived at the shop, he could smell the distinct aroma of aerosol paint and then heard the hiss of a spray can.

Terry's son, Boomer, handled all the shop marketing, silk-screening T-shirts, printing and distributing fliers, running ads for the shop, and keeping the name alive in the motorcycling community.

Club brothers used the shop as a place to meet and repair their motorcycles. It was also a place where they could get away from families, but the shop created its own family atmosphere.

As street gangs flourished, tagging and graffiti became an issue in the Los Angeles suburb smack in the middle of the L.A. basin, surrounded by freeways and 30 or 40 other suburbs, such as Whittier, South Whittier, West Whittier, Montebell, La Puente, and El Monte to the north, and La Mirada to the south.

One shiny southern California morning, as Terry arrived at the shop, he could smell the distinct aroma of aerosol paint and then heard the hiss of a spray can. He went to investigate and discovered a lanky kid on top of his fence leaning precariously toward the side of his building to deliver his tagging message. Terry charged.

The kid had a partner who immediately beat feet out of harm's way, leaving his buddy to fend for himself. Terry yanked the kid off the fence and dragged him into the shop.

"You've got a choice to make, kid," Terry said. "You can clean up and paint the side of my building or I'm calling your folks."

"Are you going to call the cops?" the frightened kid asked, shuddering in his Converse All-Star tennis shoes, Levi's, and paint-stained white T-shirt.

"We'll see," Terry said. Terry dug out all his cleaning gear, paint, and rollers. The kid quickly went to work prepping and painting the damaged area.

"Will that do it, sir?" the kid asked as Terry inspected his workmanship.

"Are you attending school?" Terry asked.

"Yes, sir," the kid quickly responded.

"I want you to go to school," Terry instructed. "But I want you to come by here every day around five. I want you to see how this shop works, and how folks make a living in their shops that you want to fuck up with your tagging."

The kid agreed and came by the shop at 5:00 p.m. He swept the sidewalk and cleaned the counters. Day after day, the kid—his name was Joaquin Fernandez—came to the shop and helped out. After a couple of weeks, his folks showed up at noon with a basket of burritos and tamales for the shop crew.

"Thank you for giving our son a break," the father said.

"Let's keep him in school," Terry said.

Joaquin watched motorcycles come together every afternoon as he arrived at the shop for his cleaning duties. He watched Terry build one bike after another. One in particular caught his attention, a yellow chopper with ghosted pearl-white flames, with chromed ape-hanger handlebars and a five-inch extended glide front end. The beautiful Softail chopper glistened as Terry rolled it into the sun. He was admiring it when a customer, a tattoo artist named Bobby Gonzales, approached.

"When will it be finished?" Gonzales asked, staring at the chromed-out, Evolution-powered, fat bob chopper in the afternoon sunlight.

"In couple of days, but it needs to be broken in," Terry explained.

"What do you want for it?" Bobby asked.

> "I want you to go to school," Terry instructed. "But I want you to come by here everyday around five. I want you to see how this shop works, and how folks make a living in their shops that you want to fuck up with your tagging."

Terry's first new Harley-Davidson, in 1993. After 20 years of building bikes and selling them to raise bail money, he finally was able to afford a new Softail.

Joaquin had acquired discipline, integrity, and brotherhood at the Triple T shop. He learned from the master.

"I hadn't thought about selling it," Terry said, "but I'll take $18,000."

Bobby nodded, eyed the chromed, spoked wheels, the 180 rear Avon tire, the bobbed yellow rear fender, and billet controls, and then left the shop. Two days passed and he was back.

"When will you start it?" Bobby asked.

"In a couple of hours," Terry said and continued his tuning procedure.

Two hours later, while Joaquin swept the shop, Bobby showed up with his girlfriend and a briefcase full of cash.

"But I haven't road-tested it," Terry said.

"How does she run?" Bobby asked.

"Like a dream," Terry said.

Bobby handed over $18,000 in cash and nodded to his girlfriend, who took off. The tattoo artist straddled the fresh motorcycle.

"Where are you going?" Terry said.

"Las Vegas," Bobby said. He rapped the pipes, dropped the clutch, and peeled out of the strip mall onto the 605 freeway heading north to Interstate 10, then the 15 toward Vegas, 257 miles away.

Joaquin witnessed the passion in a man's eyes as he straddled the bike of his dreams and rode into the desert.

Bobby rode the chopper to his tattoo parlor, Sin City, in Vegas, spent a couple of weeks riding around the sinful town, then rode the ground-up custom bike back to Triple T Choppers.

"Have any problems? Terry asked

"Not one," Bobby said, beaming from ear to ear. "I need it serviced and the oil changed. I'm riding to Chicago tomorrow.

As Terry became more confident in Joaquin's work ethic, the job duties for the fifteen-year-old expanded to answering the phones and watching the counter. The kid stayed in school but stopped over every night to see which new bike Terry was building, including a bare-bones 1958 Panhead basket case restored to a show-ready ride. A wealthy Asian stock broker had the basket case shipped to Terry's shop because he didn't want his wife to see it.

Terry made sure Joaquin stayed in school, kept his grades strong, and his folks continued to supply a hearty Mexican lunch from time to time. A couple of years passed and Joaquin graduated from Los Altos High School and enrolled in the Cerritos Junior College, gaining knowledge and a solid work ethic while continuing his work at Triple T Choppers.

Terry continued to work with the stock broker, who drove a shiny new Bentley. He restored the basket case and his customer shipped it to Japan. More projects were delivered to Triple T for ultimate export to Japan. Terry built bikes for Zeke, a shop owner in Hollywood, who in turn sold them to Hollywood elite, including Billy Idol and Lorenzo Lamas.

Finally Joaquin graduated from college with a degree in criminal law and joined the Los Angeles Sheriff's Department. A strange conclusion for someone who started out tagging garages, but Joaquin had acquired discipline, integrity, and brotherhood at the Triple T shop. He learned from the master. 💀

Drugs and Death

THE TRANSITION FROM THE 1980S TO THE 1990S was a rough one for bikers in general, and for one-percenters in particular. The world was changing and personal freedom was disappearing. Being a one-percenter was primarily about the pursuit of freedom at all costs, and the restrictive 1990s and the outlaw motorcycle club community were not a good match.

For Terry it was a time of massive change at all levels. On the personal front he was dealing with his on-again, off-again relationship with Pam. As the 1990s approached, Terry and Pam spent more time together. He would fly to Grass Valley from time to time and Pam would return to the city, and even attended club events with Terry. It all seemed mature and adult. They had already known each other and shared a positive family life for more than three decades. Pam knew the Vagos culture and respected Terry's leadership role. She enjoyed escapes to Hawaii as much as Terry. Terry enjoyed Pam's love of animals and nurturing character, but he couldn't move to Grass Valley or to her ranch in southern Oregon.

But in 1991, they decided to wed in a massive, star-studded Grass Valley extravaganza. More than 1,000 brothers traveled from as far away as Japan and Mexico to attend the gala event. The celebration was a crowning achievement, but the marriage didn't have a

Being a one-percenter was primarily about the pursuit of freedom at all costs, and the restrictive 1990s and the outlaw motorcycle club community were not a good match.

prayer. Even during their Hawaiian Island honeymoon, Terry recognized the lack of chemistry. It was as if two siblings tried to wed for protection and a myriad of other comforting, practical, and secure reasons.

After they recognized their inability to make the marriage work, Pam often asked Terry to return, but Terry knew better. "I knew I'd end up killing someone over her," Terry said. Still they remained friends right up until a car accident on Indian Wells Road in Grass Valley took Pam's life in 2010.

On the club front things were even more chaotic. As Terry and the Vagos moved into the 1990s and their court case raged on, Terry grappled with leading the baddest club in Southern California, or at least attempting to lead them, trying to keep members out of jail and afford them some rights in the growing asphalt jungle of 10 million, all while attempting to be a responsible family man.

His life was a swirling mixture of violent circumstance, contradicting personalities, and diverse social elements. He wanted to be a

Monster Red, a Berdoo member of the Vagos, standing on Rosarita beach, near Tijuana, Mexico. The big man wears Vago green with pride and the recently reformed Vago patch. Terry worked to make the gargoyle more distinctive and the center patch more resilient in 1990.

good father and keep a decent, well-kept home, but the unlit side of his moon contained torn leathers, oil-soaked Levi's, fights to the death, and territorial wars. One day he mowed his lawn;

One drug after another sent bikers into jail cells or coffins.

the next night, he relied on the killer sitting next to him to watch his back while sizing up the sonuvabitch across the table who wanted to kill him.

The whole notion of outlaw organizations wearing affiliated patches changed drastically from the 1970s to the 1990s. One drug after another sent bikers into jail cells or coffins.

"PCP and Cannabidiol (horse tranquilizer) nearly wrecked this club," Terry said. Cannabidiol—CBD—is a cannabinoid found in marijuana—it is the "canna" in "cannabis." It has a sedative effect and has been used as an animal tranquilizer, but it can also increase alertness. It relieves convulsion, inflammation, anxiety, and nausea, and it inhibits cancer cell growth. It has also been proven to work as an antipsychotic for the treatment of schizophrenia and may reduce the growth of aggressive human breast cancer cells. It also gets the user higher than shit.

PCP has an even more potent intoxicating effect, but doesn't have any of the positive benefits and is only used to tranquilize animals . . . and bikers. Use of both PCP and CBD reached epidemic proportions among members of motorcycle clubs in the 1970s and '80s. In this regard, the Vagos were no exception to the rule. When the buzz of horse tranquilizers wore off, the club shifted to costly cocaine, then bennies, but ultimately cheaply cooked methamphetamine took over.

"I initiated a zero-tolerance effort," Terry said. "If you got caught on drugs you were gone. Drugs took everything. Some brothers sold their motorcycles for a pinch."

During the 1990s, the Vagos wasn't the only organization battling bad cops. Clubs had run amok for a couple of decades, and police all over the nation were leaning on the hard-riding madmen. Too often they twisted laws or tossed them out the window as they dealt with bikers, and one-percenter clubs in particular.

> The surviving club members had watched brothers fall prey to drugs, bad busts, beatings by cops, and unlawful searches and seizures.

As club members reached their thirties, some semblance of the survival instinct started to kick in. The surviving club members had watched brothers fall prey to drugs, bad busts, beatings by cops, and unlawful searches and seizures. Those activities prevented outlaws from moving around freely without harassment, even in their hometowns.

The biker magazine, *Easyriders*, started a grassroots organization, ABATE (A Brotherhood Against Totalitarian Enactments) in the early 1970s. This forerunner of the motorcycle rights movement grew into a rough rabble of legislatively active state organizations across the country. By the mid-1980s, more than 30,000 uneducated bikers in twenty-eight states were learning the ways of politics through ABATE chapters. State leaders knew their local elected officials by first name. Outlaws, who generally shunned any connection to straight society, were forced to learn to protect their own rights. The Vagos's Hawthorne case proved enlightening and built confidence on the streets. The bikers were learning the ways of the Man.

In January 1986, an attorney named Richard Lester established the National Coalition of Motorcyclists (NCOM) to accomplish two goals: afford a national forum for state motorcycle rights groups to share information about helmet laws, restrictive legislation, and rights violations, and to form of a nationwide network of attorneys, linking them to groups of prospective customers all over the country. It worked, to the chagrin of some hardcore motorcyclists who didn't care for the connection to a group of ambulance-chasing attorneys. On the other hand, as the organization was accepted and the network of attorneys grew, more and more legal minds stepped forward to help motorcycle rights advocates on a pro-bono basis.

Terry followed the progress of Richard's business model on the pages of motorcycle magazines, and because he was based near Lester's Van Nuys office, they came in contact from time to time.

In February of 1990, the Vagos had won a $2 million court settlement against the Hawthorne Police Department and club brothers across the country were beginning to feel the empowerment and strength, like a group of immigrants who had been mistreated but finally received citizenship.

But they hadn't collected their court settlement yet. In May of 1990, a headline in the South Bay Edition of the *LA Times* read, "Two Insurers Balk at Hawthorne's Debt to Motorcyclists Liability: City may have to pay part of $1.95-million settlement to members of the Vagos motorcycle club."

According to Terry, the judge told the Hawthorne city attorneys at the conclusion of the trial, "They (Vagos) will own your town if you don't pay quickly. Get your policies and come to my chambers."

Hawthorne authorities were scared at the prospect of having to cover the settlement. Two insurance companies battled over which one should pay. One insurance carrier filed a lawsuit against the city and the other bobbed and weaved. Insurance reserves were rapidly depleting under the constant police problems with individuals in their city, and the PD's use of excessive force was costing them dearly. The city coverage called for insurance coverage for each occurrence under the terms of the insurance program, and they were attempting to use the small print to dodge this significant bullet.

"We hope the insurance companies don't abandon us, because we could not afford to pay the whole amount ourselves," said City Manager Kenneth Jue.

Canadian Insurance Company of Costa Mesa, California, the primary city liability carrier, noted that their policy required no more than a $1 million payment be made for a single occurrence. Since they determined the entire Vagos case to be a single occurrence, their liability did not exceed 1 million.

The secondary insurance carrier, Protective National Insurance Company of Omaha, Nebraska, contended that each violation of human rights was a separate occurrence and Canadian should be responsible for the entire $1.95 million settlement.

"It was obvious to me and Protective National that the case against the city of Hawthorne constitutes multiple occurrences, at

The judge told the Hawthorne city attorneys at the conclusion of the trial, "They (Vagos) will own your town if you don't pay quickly."

least, more than two," said Lance Orloff, an attorney for Protective National.

Of course Orloff also complained about the timing of the settlement. He didn't like being notified so close to the conclusion of the case.

"(Hawthorne attorneys) thought they were going to win the case in the beginning," Orloff said. "Protective National wasn't even given notice that the lawsuit was going on and that the city was in trouble until, all of a sudden, they called up and said, 'Gee, the witnesses aren't going as well as we thought they would.'

"Every time the police went out and destroyed someone's property, that was an additional occurrence," Orloff said. "The evidence admitted during the trial indicated that police had a long history of going after the motorcycle gang, for whatever reasons."

Protective had a poor track record and financial difficulties of their own, and dodged involvement in other cities, including a $5.5 million judgment in Torrance, which they refused to pay. The city became restless and afraid they would be caught with the bill.

An appeal was put forth and payment was delayed in Torrance, although Torrance threatened to sue Protective.

The slime balls began to surface as far away as Nebraska, with Protective financial problems stemming back to the mid-1980s. The Nebraska Insurance Department was monitoring Protective's operations. In December of 1989, they had a surplus of $18.9 million, which was slipping rapidly, and Nebraska officials were attempting to maintain its solvency.

The parent company, Central National Insurance of Omaha, faced additional desperate circumstances. Earlier in May of 1990, Nebraska insurance officials took over day-to-day operations. It wasn't looking good for the plaintiffs in the Vagos case.

"Ultimately, we were paid," said Terry the Tramp. "I think the state stepped in."

In several groups, members of the group of plaintiffs were called to the ACLU offices in a seedy industrial section of downtown Los Angeles to pick up individual checks of $21,000 apiece. For Terry it was far less than the actual funds he raised personally to cover the initial legal fees, or the value of his time, but it was worth it for the club.

Said Terry of the settlement, "Everybody got to buy a new car."

Through the 1980s clubs had learned that they weren't the only bad-asses on the block, that cheats and miscreants flourished all over the planet in the form of insurance executives, cops, and police chiefs.

In June of 1992, Terry and the Southern California Vagos tested their knowledge of the law when they sued an Anaheim bar. The bar instituted a dress code that prohibited "motorcycle attire." Nineteen Vago members sued the Loose Moose Saloon on Katella Avenue, claiming they violated the Unruh Civil Rights Act, which prohibits arbitrary discrimination by a business.

In early 1991, the bar owner, David Koontz, who was a part of a Nevada-based corporation, posted a "No motorcycle attire allowed" sign, denying Vagos entry. Wearing club colors was also mentioned by employees as a reason for keeping Vagos out.

The club sued and successfully forced the restaurant chain to relinquish the dress code, and the court awarded the Vagos a meager settlement of $1,600, which Terry and his brothers gave to the National Coalition of Motorcyclists to support future efforts by Richard Lester's growing motorcycle rights group. Club brothers were learning the legal way of the land.

Harley-Davidson had an impact with its new, more reliable Evolution engine, and by the late eighties, more and more clubbers were riding across the country. ☠

Expansion Pitfalls

TERRY THE TRAMP HAD A GROWING REPUTATION as a hard-line bad-ass. The Vagos were his life, his mission, and his family. In 1988, he turned 41, a treacherous age for any man, a time of questioning, rampant ambition, and personal searching. But Terry didn't have much time for deep, introspective thought processes and questioning. He was now the international president of a rapidly growing organization of supposed criminals and thugs. Between busts, raids, fights, disputes with other clubs, and his son, he had precious little time for soul searching. Ambition was the order of the day for many clubs and fending off challenges was almost like a full-time job.

Motorcycle clubs faced a turning point. They'd run ragged for a couple of decades, but now they confronted drastic and sometimes

This photo was taken at the 1994 National Coalition of Motorcyclists annual meeting, in Harrisburg, Pennsylvania. From the left: Randy, from the Sons of Hawaii MC, Moth Eater from the Pagans MC, Terry the Tramp, Chico from the Dirty Dozen, and an unknown rider from Germany.

life-threatening decisions. The knife-edge existence of the competitive motorcycle outlaw club was sharp. Some one-percenter clubs spread across the country and around the world. Others chose to remain one-chapter organizations. Some clubs chose to challenge themselves to be a part of the one-percenter ranks; others chose to become lighter-weight groups, family clubs, Christian, community, or even touring groups. Some clubs chose to make money illegally and become full-blown criminal organizations: pimps, drug runners, meth cookers—you name it.

Terry's group resided in the center of the West Coast action. Facing opposite the club was the growing law enforcement footprint, with seriously expanding budgets, actively inflating powers, increased use of technology, and their prosecutors' scorecards. Thanks to the dictatorial powers given to law enforcement by the RICO Act, the shoe making that footprint was starting to resemble a jackboot.

> **Ambition was the order of the day for many clubs and fending off challenges was almost like a full-time job.**

Law enforcement sought any means to break down a brotherhood, and snitches proved to be the most expedient tool. When law enforcement agencies arrested any club member, they'd immediately try to pressure him into snitching, telling him if he snitched he could avoid serving jail time. It became an absurd and dangerous cycle, and an extremely ineffectual police practice. Only the weak ratted on brothers. The cycle ended when they arrested someone with too much integrity to snitch. Cops always threatened to throw the book at club members, even for the most minor crimes, but if the brothers held up and didn't snitch, the courts would ultimately take the case out of the hands of law enforcement, and every brother would have his say in front of a judge.

In 1994, a young member of the Vagos, Spike, opened Custom Cycle Creations, a small bike shop in Riverside near the suburb of Rubidoux. He was just a three-year member of the San Fernando Valley Chapter, but he'd grown up in the club world.

"He was the driving force behind the Vagos," Spike said of Terry. "The club was changing and different types of folks were coming into the club. Terry was the boss and I watched from a distance."

Spike had a full-time regular job as a Frito Lay fleet mechanic for fourteen years, but he injured himself on the job and collected disability payments, which afforded him additional time to tinker with Harleys in his garage. He was excited at the prospect of running his own shop and helping his brothers.

While setting up his small business in the Rubidoux Industrial Park, he met a middle-aged biker named Flash at U.S. Enterprises, a custom shop in Ontario.

"He was a skinny, dope-fiend looking sort, working in the service department," Spike recalled. "I needed a part and no one was manning the counter, so I stepped into the service area, and this scrawny guy helped me out."

When he opened his shop, Spike contacted Flash for parts. The forty-year-old Flash lost his job at the Ontario shop and started to come around more often with deals and bikes for sale. Spike's shop business grew, and they helped bikers all over the blistering-hot Riverside area. Spike tried to learn from Terry, who had a knack for sizing up strangers.

"He had an aura about him," Spike said. "He was a cautious man. I wished I had picked up that aspect of Tramp's forceful character."

Spike leased out an industrial space in the middle row of shops toward the back of the business park, planted against the Pomona freeway's protective 30-foot gradient, covered in slick ice plant. He hired Flash to hang fluorescent shop lights and run copper tubing for compressed air to the service lifts. The shop kicked off and business started to flow his way.

"He started to come around more and opened up to us," Spike said. "He told us he was a retired Mongol. I knew he was a drug fiend. We started calling him 'Snortin' Norton.'"

"He had an aura about him," Spike said. "He was a cautious man. I wished I had picked up that aspect of Tramp's forceful character."

Flash, always in a jam, drove a rental car and needed help with the payment or he couldn't make it to work on time. Spike fronted him the cash. Flash lived in a rundown motel with his drug-addict wife and three young boys.

"They were a freaky team," Spike said of the destitute couple.

Flash showed up at the motel one afternoon and discovered his ol' lady jawing with a stranger. He went off on her and slapped her in the parking lot. When one of his sons intervened, he slugged the kid. A witness called 911.

Spike received a desperate call.

"I got busted for assault," Flash blurted from the Riverside county jail. "Can you bail me out? I gotta get out of here."

It was a Thursday and the shop wasn't rolling in bags of coin just yet. Spike was short on cash and couldn't raise bail money for this scurvy loner, a part-time employee, at the drop of a hat.

"I tried," Spike said, "but I couldn't move fast enough."

Two days later, Flash showed up at the shop and did a massive rail of crank, or speed, on the glass of the shop's counter display.

"I told 'em I was going to commit suicide if they didn't let me out of there," Flash said and went back to work.

"I wish I studied the Tramp more closely," Spike said. "With Flash there was always a deal that was too good to be true."

Spike's business stepped up. More bikes showed up for work or for sale. The deals were too easy and lucrative, and Spike's bank account expanded.

Flash was being paid $300 a week by the cops and promised $20,000 on completion of a successful investigation.

Suddenly, Flash announced that he was opening his own polishing shop in nearby Riverside off Blaine Road. Just as unpredictably, he showed up with a new U-haul van to deliver bikes and parts to his new facility.

"I'll never forget the day a Mongol MC member stepped into our showroom," Spike said. "As soon as he heard Flash's high-pitched, nasally voice, he eyes lit up. I should have known."

Flash wasn't a retired Mongol, but a member who had ripped off his brothers and was unceremoniously kicked out of the club. As it turned out, the fully equipped motorcycle parts polishing shop was adjacent to a fully operational police investigation unit. All the phones in the shop were tapped and cameras were installed throughout the facility, leading next door to a bank of monitors watched by officers. All the components or motorcycles delivered to Flash's facility were photographed and documented.

Flash was being paid $300 a week by the cops and promised $20,000 on completion of a successful investigation. He was also making bank off the law enforcement-paid-for shop. He was working both sides of the system, searching for hot deals for Spike, his brothers, and members of other clubs in the region. On the other side of the wall, he promised Froge, the lead undercover biker and investigator, a massive assault on the region's one-percenter outlaw organizations, including the Vagos, Mongols, Hells Angels, and Hessians. Spike was unexpectedly at the forefront.

For months the shifty, scraggly, sunken-eyed speed freak worked the bikers, while promising law enforcement vast, far-reaching arrests into the very core of the outlaw community, including the highest leadership positions. That led straight to Terry the Tramp, the international president of the Vagos.

On a bright and sunny 20th of May, 1996, Spike's wife, Tammy, stepped out onto the porch of their Moreno Valley home at 6:00 a.m. and stretched before her morning walk around the pristine, upscale neighborhood. A tight, 125-pound, redhead who never saw the light of day without makeup and her hair perfectly positioned over her bright facial features, she briskly rounded the corner, and came face-to-face with members of twenty-one county and state agencies positioned to raid Spike's home.

"They snatched her up," Spike said. "They were prepared for an all out fire-fight with me. My wife told them, 'Relax, just call him. He'll come out.' "

Flash had told the officers that Spike was primed for a running gun battle from an armed-to-the-teeth fortress full of machine guns and heavy artillery. Instead, they rolled on a comfortable middle-

For months the shifty, scraggly, sunken-eyed speed freak worked the bikers, while promising law enforcement vast, far-reaching arrests into the very core of the outlaw community, including the highest leadership positions.

class neighborhood with manicured lawns and decent, frightened citizens. Spike was instructed to remove his shirt and shoes and come out of his house, while his neighbors stood and watched from their adjacent lawns.

Cops from myriad agencies stormed his home and thirty-nine other locations throughout Southern California. On that warm morning, while Spike sat in the back of a blistering hot black and white police unit, additional members of the 400-strong assault force busted and arrested thirty-two of thirty-five suspects in Pasadena, Azusa, Pomona, West Covina, El Monte, Rosemead, Glendora, and Shadow Hills in LA County. Raids also took place in Santa Ana Heights and Yorba Linda in Orange County, where supplementary warrants were served.

"I was on the list," Terry said. "Spike brought Flash over to my house once, but I wouldn't let him stay. I didn't like that punk. He smelled bad."

The Riverside County DA, Grover Trask, brimmed with pride as the undercover investigation unfolded on a hot Inland Valley day. "We found out how they were doing business," he said. "We broke the code of silence."

They tracked the flow of stolen motorcycle parts and insurance scams amounting to $4 million, and were able to indict members of the notorious Vagos, Mongols, Hessians, and Hells Angels affiliates.

At Spike's shop the cops gathered up a dozen Harleys in various states of reconditioning. Some were reduced to bare frames and they discovered two examples of altered vehicle identification numbers.

According to the *LA Times*, outlaw motorcyclists all over Southern California were conspiring to steal Harleys or stage thefts to perpetuate insurance fraud. They apparently sold bikes to Japan and used the legitimate numbers again on stolen domestic models. The sealed indictment alleged thirty-five counts of stolen property, fifteen counts of altering numbers, three counts of assault with a deadly weapon, and one count each of robbery, kidnapping, and torture. The shit hit the fan, coupled with allegations of operating chop shops and distributing methamphetamine.

Terry was an ace in the hole for Flash and Froge, as they promoted their crime spree effort internally.

"You've got to nail Tramp," Froge told the slippery snitch. If they could take down the international president of one of the most notorious clubs in the nation, they would become heroes in the law enforcement community.

> ## "You've got to nail Tramp," Froge told the slippery snitch.

The morning of the bust a call came from his son, Terry the Wall, from his home. "The cops were here, Dad," he said. "They're on their way to your shop."

Terry knew exactly what was coming down, but he thought it would be best for him and anyone involved in the raid if he could stay on the streets and deal with the legal ramifications. He scrambled to lock the small shop and jumped into his El Camino. He knew his shop was clean, but he couldn't vouch for every used part stashed in the back.

As he scrambled for the pickup out front, he could hear the sirens screaming in the distance. Undercover cars slammed onto his street as he peeled out of sight. Riverside agents stormed his shop, waving a warrant listing eighty charges for the leader of the Vagos, but they didn't have warrants to search his shop. That didn't stop them. They pried open the door, but after a complete search of his facility by dozens of officers, only two insignificant motorcycle components, a front end and a transmission, were taken into evidence.

Terry stayed on the streets for two weeks, working with bail bondsmen and attorneys. Finally, with his bail bondsman and attorney at his side, he turned himself in. While waiting for court, Terry was put in a holding tank in the Riverside County jail. Only one other individual shared the cell. The scrawny kid with long hair and shifty eyes moved as far from Terry as he could. The punk spotted Spike in the adjacent cell and signaled for him to come over.

"You've got to get me out of this cell," he said to Spike, visibly trembling. "If [Terry] finds out I'm Flash's cousin, I'm done for."

There wasn't much Spike could do, but the young man's fearful eyes told him how unrelenting Flash's snitch efforts had become. He had busted his own relatives.

Spike shook his head and leaned close to the bars. "Just keep your mouth shut."

> **As he scrambled for the pickup out front, he could hear the sirens screaming in the distance. Undercover cars slammed onto his street as he peeled out of sight.**

Terry, the IP of the Vagos, was unceremoniously shackled and escorted into court. The courtroom was packed with cops. His photo was flashed in the cold hall, along with photographs of Sonny Barger. They presented Terry as if he was the John Gotti of the outlaw motorcycle world.

"My attorney, Terrence P. Dobins, stuck with me as they read the indictments, and argued on my behalf as the judge set the bail at $2 million," Terry said.

"The original DA was a smart ass," Terry said. "I called her a bitch. She got fired and the judge was moved to another court before the case resumed."

Terry began a lengthy effort to raise funds for his own defense. The club supplied $6,000 of the $300,000 he was forced to muster for the defense of more than 186 felony counts. Sixteen bank accounts were frozen and two prosecutors were assigned to the follow-up investigation.

Once all the shit went down and Terry was behind bars, the pressure was on. Families fell apart. Club members who didn't have the heart for this level of scrutiny headed for the hills. During the investigation, the City of Los Angeles wrote a letter to the Riverside investigators. "We spent $1.5 million investigating Terry Orendorff," the letter read. "We never found anything."

"We hoped all forty defendants would hang together and demand a jury trial," Spike said. "The [DA's] case was weak, and if we all stormed the courtroom with our attorneys, we had a serious shot."

The district attorney's office, headed by Mark McDonald, scrambled to make deals by offering probation to some of the lesser-charged individuals. Mark eventually brought about his own undoing. He left the district attorney's office and opened a private practice, ultimately defending Vagos members.

"I suspected that some guys were going to flip to save their asses," said Spike.

As probation deals surfaced and some defendants began to walk, Flash panicked. Between his lies and promised arrests, and the DA's assurance to put everyone away for a long time behind Flash's allegations, he felt safe until he watched Vagos walk out of the courthouse, free.

He stormed the DA's office and started to picket the Riverside courthouse sidewalk with a makeshift plaque, hoping to draw media attention.

"He used his wife and kids," Terry said. "They were scared to death. Even the kids carried makeshift placards on wooden poles outside the courtroom on the hot summer Riverside sidewalk."

Spike's attorney noticed the commotion in the halls and called their investigators, two former LA cops. They swept Flash up and stuck him in a conference room, where they questioned him for four hours and taped every minute. Flash was the ultimate lowlife. He immediately turned on the cops and spilled his guts about the false evidence, overworked charges, and bad deals.

The information was surreptitiously leaked to the DA's office and the case rapidly disintegrated. Spike was able to take the unprovoked bullshit rap off his wife, and they cut her loose. His son was given a mere two years probation.

"I loaned him $1,000 to bail his son out," Terry said.

Terry's case was dropped, and Spike's case was reduced from twenty-eight years to six. Forced to take a chop-shop charge,

"We don't know where he is," Terry said, "and we don't care."

Terry and Spike, who took the fall in the 1990s behind the snitch Flash and investigator Froge's bullshit case against the Vagos and various Southern California clubs. Millions of dollars were spent on the case and thousands of man-hours wasted. Two men went to jail, and another escaped to Canada.

Spike was able to grab any charge with Terry's name on it. "I had to do whatever I could for the leader of the club," Spike said. Out of thirty-five defendants, only three went to prison, and one of those escaped to Canada. Just two of the convicted men were Vagos, and one was a Mongol. Flash and his wife and kids were transferred to Reno and sequestered into witness protection programs, their names changed. They lived there until they were spotted and Flash freaked again.

Not that he had anything to worry about. "We don't know where he is," Terry said, "and we don't care."

Snitches like Flash live in terror, a prison of their own making, trying to hide from the men they tried to destroy for personal gain, or to avoid further time behind bars. There is nowhere to hide when fear consumes a man's soul.

Spike's bail was dropped from $2 million to $250,000 during the case, and he bailed out of Riverside County. He dealt with the case for seven months then returned to Riverside for sentencing.

He was bussed to Tehachapi for processing and ultimately to Chuckawalla State Prison in Blythe, California, at the desert border with Arizona on Interstate 10 and highway 95. Blythe was synonymous with "bleak," in the middle of nowhere California in the Colorado section of the Sonora Desert. During the wettest Blythe year in a century, the dreary area received just over 8.7 inches of rain in 1951. In 1956, it rained only 0.18 inches for a blistering drought.

Spike's prison bus rolled off the freeway and he witnessed his last California greenery before the desert sands of Arizona, and Yuma, 95 miles to the south. It was as dry as a popcorn fart as the bus rumbled west of Blythe in unincorporated Riverside County toward the reasonably new, level II, medium-security prison facility opened in 1988. It covered 1,720 acres, and although it was designed to house 1,738 prisoners it was already overpopulated. Primary housing consisted of eleven open dormitory-styled buildings on four main yards.

General population inmates in the five-yard facility were allowed to enter and leave their living quarters as they wished, except at night, during count times, or during lockdown procedures.

Spike was assigned to the level II secure yard and told the gang coordinator and his counselor, "I want to make good use of my time." They referred him to the warden's committee, but for his first year he received only tension from the staff because they deemed him part of a disruptive group. "They expected problems from me," Spike said.

He read and studied for his GED exam. Once that was behind him, he stepped up again and asked to work with kids. Doors gradually opened and he was approved for level I by the warden's committee and given the opportunity to counsel kids. Then through his own efforts to be progressive, he was given the chance to work at the fire station and study for various levels of fire service. He received his Fire 1 certification, and then Fire 2 level training.

The brick Chuckawalla Fire Department building resided outside the prison gates. Three fire engineers and the Chuckawalla fire chief managed the facility with twelve prison interns.

"It was the best job on the post," Spike said. "If you fucked up there, you were done."

The firehouse duties included all prison building fires, and assisting county units with runs to the freeway to pull folks from burning cars.

Later in life while counseling his daughter, Spike told her, "I always wanted to be a fireman. That was my plan until your mother got pregnant at seventeen, and I was forced to go to work. It wasn't until I was imprisoned that I had the opportunity to reach my goal."

It was too late for Spike, though. He was forty-four and too old to apply at any fire department, his criminal record notwithstanding.

"Tramp would be there for me," Spike said. "He would help me get a job, get settled, and although I was on parole, I would still be supported by the Vagos."

"I met one lifer inside who told me something that always stuck," Spike said. "He told me not to make this place a revolving door. I took that to heart."

As he departed the prison in 2001 with his wife and his son at his side, he immediately noticed the lack of respect by citizens on the streets.

"I couldn't wait for a good meal." As he rolled into a Coco's restaurant, just off the 10 Interstate, he immediately observed the lack of consideration offered by youngsters.

"Everything was about respect in prison," Spike said. "You didn't get up from the dinner table unless you excused yourself. It was all about courtesy and reverence."

As he ordered his first meal of freedom, Spike was certain about one aspect of his new life on the outside.

"Tramp would be there for me," Spike said. "He would help me get a job, get settled, and although I was on parole, I would still be supported by the Vagos."

"I would do anything I could to help a brother out," Terry said.

The Evil Tentacles of Growth

THE VAGOS HAD SURVIVED ANOTHER MAJOR law enforcement onslaught. The government continually grew more evil fangs and sharpened their growing ivory tusks with the fine stones of criminal technology and enhanced legislative powers, but their rat operators were always the weak link.

During the time Terry had been a member of the Vagos, all clubs underwent drastic demographic changes. Like the rest of America, these groups of asphalt nomads were aging; they were no longer twenty-year-old warriors straddling straight-pipe Harleys. Their short list of priorities had grown and no longer consisted of just owning a motorcycle and getting laid. Who cared about owning a home or even a car in the 1960s? By the time members hit their forties, their priorities had changed. Some wanted to own homes,

Vagos on the set of the Morton Downey Show, Palm Springs, in 1989. From left, Little Joe, Terry's son, Junkie Ed, Thirty-Seven, Hessian George, Sonny Bono, Terry, and David.

cars, even TVs. They wanted more than just a six-pack and a new woman on Friday night. They wanted to ride across the country, stay in motels, and buy souvenirs. Times were changing again.

In 1998, Terry became aware of two members of other, smaller southern California clubs who had approached Richard to develop an organization to protect the rights of club members. Richard, a short, unassuming, unpretentious, mild-mannered motorcyclist with curly black hair and a salt-and-pepper beard, looked like a Jewish accountant. He didn't fit the tough, tall, biker mold, but he had a soft spot for motorcycling, along with the balls to step into the treacherous arena of one-percenters.

"I told Richard this effort was beyond what he thought he was capable of," said Pepper Massey, the executive director of NCOM for ten years. "But when Richard was determined, nothing would stop him." Dealing with one chapter of one club was treacherous enough, but multiply that to twenty or thirty clubs, and the risk was tremendous.

At the forefront of the effort was James Bondo, a long-haired, light-hearted, outspoken member of the Monks MC from Azusa, California, and Quaff "Party" Dave, the president of the Quaffs MC.

"I was an MMA (Modified Motorcycle Association) rep in the mid-eighties," Bondo said. "I was dealing with cop problems constantly. Club members were getting slaughtered on the streets. We were continually pulled over for no probable cause, just because we wore a patch."

Bondo took on the job of sharing the notion of a confederation with clubs all over Southern California at runs, at parties at the Monk clubhouse, and at meetings with various clubs.

> **Dealing with one chapter of one club was treacherous enough, but multiply that to twenty or thirty clubs, and the risk was tremendous.**

"It wasn't always fun," said Bondo, "but brothers were beginning to listen."

"When Vagos and Hessians came to the table for the first time," Pepper Massey said, "other clubs stepped up."

"Jesse" James Bondo from the Monks MC was the first person to approach Terry about organizing the clubs into an alliance, which took some guts on Bondo's part. Many club guys were intimidated by Terry's swaggering and by his position within the Vagos, but Bondo's passion for motorcycling and freedom superceded any club pushing and shoving. He approached Terry, whom he had known for a decade, at the monthly Costa Mesa swap meet on a hot summer day. Terry was surrounded by members of the green machine, but the patchholder from the Monks motorcycle club approached the boss and asked for a minute of his time.

Bondo explained the situation. Clubs had become the focal point for increased police harassment and Bondo believed the clubs needed to band together to find a solution. He was preaching to the boss of the choir; this was a message that Terry had long been trying to get across to anyone who would listen. Hearing a similar message from a like-minded member of a different club piqued Terry's interest. Terry knew Bondo, knew his club, and respected his desire to find a solution to increased club harassment. He knew the power of numbers, but a joint effort on the part of the various clubs would only work if club rivalries were set aside and the patchholders could communicate openly. So Terry offered to discuss the notion with his club and afterwards meet with Bondo for further discussion. Surrounded by club members and garage vendors selling their dented chrome and rusting wares, Bondo and Terry opened a dialogue that would eventually benefit members of motorcycle clubs around the world.

A meeting was set for a couple of weeks out, at a conference room at the West Covina Holiday Inn. Prior to the meeting Terry contacted several clubs in his Southern California region, spread the word, and asked for leadership attendance. That warm evening, brothers from the Righteous Ones, The Monks, the Sundowners, the Tribe, the Hessians, the Nuggets, the Humpers, Set Free, and the Vietnam Vets MC rolled into the parking lot just off Interstate 10. Some of the clubs in attendance didn't get along, but they were guaranteed safe passage to and from the meeting.

"For the first time, I met Richard Lester," Terry said. "I quickly determined that he was an ambulance-chasing attorney and called him on it."

Richard, with rough features and a graying beard, was shorter than Terry. He didn't look like an attorney or a biker. It was as if he didn't fit either mold, and his ability to carry on a conversation was equally disconnected. His stumbling discourse didn't fit anyone's idea of slick lawyer's banter, nor did he strike anyone as a down-to-earth biker. His verbal communication skills were rough, but he made a vital point.

"We all listened," Terry said. "It didn't sound too bad." But the key was linked to whether Richard would keep his word.

"All the chickenshit was put aside while we discussed forming the Confederation of Clubs," Terry recalled. "We had to give it a shot. We needed the representation."

> **"All the chickenshit was put aside while we discussed forming the Confederation of Clubs," Terry recalled. "We had to give it a shot. We needed the representation."**

Terry worked with Quaff Dave and Bondo of the Monks MC, Tombstone from the Hessians, and Lester to establish the Confederation of Clubs and to enhance communication and working relations between clubs.

"Richard provided the vehicle," said Pepper Massey, "and the club members were keen to effect changes. They didn't want to sit around; they wanted to make things happen."

"Quaff Dave understood," Pepper said. "He was the peacemaker and knew if clubs worked together, they could accomplish a lot."

Popeye, the big, tough Vietnam vet, understood the vision. "He was built like a brick shithouse," Pepper said. "But he was well-respected and got it. He knew there was a lot of equity out there with the clubs if harnessed properly."

"With broader travel, the strong motorcycle rights effort, heightened communication, reliable motorcycles, more proactive attorneys, the will and synergy of the patch holder grew," said Pepper. "They were no longer forced to succumb to discrimination, no-colors rules, or harassment."

> **"Terry the Tramp was a forward-thinking member. He thought way out in front of most one-percenters."**

"When we first started the confederation," said Richard Lester, "Terry the Tramp was a forward-thinking member. He thought way out in front of most one-percenters."

At first, they would attend the meetings out of curiosity to see who would survive. Some were fearful to be in the same room with so many patches, but Southern California was the perfect proving ground. They slowly realized that this was a comfortable place, where all members could share their feelings and issues openly. They also quickly learned their collective strengths. Together they could effect change."

"For months my phone bill ran over $500," said Bondo. He was the Monks MC's political activist and was determined to grow this organization and protect his brothers from being harassed in the streets. Initially the dues were $100 per year per club, which afforded two representatives from each patch a position in the confederation.

The bylaws were simple. "No cops allowed, and you couldn't be a member if you were affiliated with law enforcement in any way," said Rusty, an active Hells Angel. "At one point, forest rangers were not allowed to join."

"Club politics were not discussed during these meetings," said Terry, "There was a neutral rule. One club could not fuck with another club before, after, or during a Confederation meeting. After the meeting, if a club had a problem with another patch, they could roll to a nearby coffee shop and discuss the issue. The notion was that this was a time of discussion and getting along."

"Unfortunately," said Bondo, "each meeting contained law enforcement spies. If an event was discussed, we knew the cops would be there."

Through the Confederation meetings club members learned how legislation was passed.

"They learned to kill bills in committee," Bondo continued. "With the help of A.I.M. attorneys (Aid to Injured Motorcyclists, the

It was not
difficult for
creative civil
attorneys
to depict
practically any
wrongdoing
as mail or
wire fraud,
enabling law
enforcement to
use RICO as a
tool against any
organization
it didn't
particularly like.

subgroup of NCOM that organized the attorneys), we learned search and seizure laws. We learned what we could and could not say to law enforcement. We learned the rights of motorcycle passengers."

Club members had a lot to learn, and a lot at stake because of the RICO gang act. In 1970, Congress passed the Racketeer Influenced and Corrupt Organizations (RICO) Act, Title 18, United States Code, Sections 1961-1968. The act defined "racketeering activity" as any act or threat involving murder, kidnapping, gambling, arson, robbery, bribery, extortion, dealing in obscene matter, or dealing in a controlled substance or listed chemical chargeable under state law; or any act that was indictable relating to bribery, counterfeiting, theft from interstate shipment, embezzlement from pension and welfare funds, extortion, fraud and related activity in connection with identification documents, section 1029 relating to fraud, gambling, mail fraud, wire fraud, financial institution fraud, obstruction of justice, obstruction of criminal investigations, obstruction of state or local law enforcement, tampering with a witness, victim, or an informant, peonage, slavery, and trafficking in persons, among other things.

Congress' stated goal was to eliminate the ill effects of organized crime on the nation's economy. In other words, RICO was intended to destroy the Mafia. Throughout the 1970s, RICO's intended purpose and its actual use didn't exactly match. Initially RICO was rarely used except in the prosecution of the Mafia, but that would change. Because of RICO's broad powers—the result of Congress' inclusion of mail and wire fraud as two crimes upon which a RICO claim could be brought—the law was ripe for potential abuse. Because of the breadth of activities that had historically been criminally prosecuted under the mail and wire fraud statutes, it was not difficult for creative civil attorneys to depict practically any wrongdoing as mail or wire fraud, enabling law enforcement to use RICO as a tool against any organization it didn't particularly like.

By the 1980s, law enforcement had discovered that the RICO act could be used as a tool to prosecute virtually any group, such as street gangs or motorcycle clubs. Instead of being used as a tool to prosecute the Mafia, RICO was used to prosecute individuals, businesses, clubs, gangs, political protest groups, and terrorist organizations. It was easy for law enforcement to get outrageous sentences for members of motorcycle clubs by prosecuting them under the RICO Act in virtually any context. Law enforcement used the RICO Act to take down entire clubs. To make matters worse, the RICO Act allowed law enforcement to take any member's funding, which prevented him from obtaining valid defense. The law states:

> It shall be unlawful for any person who has received any income derived, directly or indirectly, from a pattern of racketeering activity or through collection of an unlawful debt in which such person has participated as a principal within the meaning of section 2, title 18, United States Code, to use or invest, directly or indirectly, any part of such income, or the proceeds of such income, in acquisition of any interest in, or the establishment or operation of, any enterprise which is engaged in, or the activities of which affect, interstate or foreign commerce.

This meant that law enforcement officials could confiscate defendant's families' businesses, and any kind of asset they could lay their hands on, virtually ensuring that the member was unable to defend himself, regardless of how weak the case against him.

At first the club members were like blind kittens playing on running table saw. Many of them had their lives completely destroyed because of trumped-up RICO charges. "They didn't have a clue," Bondo said, "but they learned."

During Confederation meetings in the garage at Bondo's corner-lot stucco home, club representatives shared information that would

During Confederation meetings in the garage at Bondo's corner-lot stucco home, club representatives shared information that would help them avoid walking into the RICO buzz saw.

help them avoid walking into the RICO buzz saw. Richard Lester and Terry the Tramp always attended.

"Club wars diminished significantly," Terry said. "The Confederation gave club brothers an open platform."

After two years, Bondo stepped down as the chairman and Hessian Tombstone became active. Tombstone was followed by Popeye, a Vietnam Vet MC member. He was still the active chairman in southern California in 2010.

"It was touch and go in the beginning," said Lester. "At the first meeting, I didn't know who was going to shoot whom."

At the first Arizona meeting, members of the Dirty Dozen came to the meeting wearing bandoliers of ammunition and carrying Uzis. It took forward-thinking leaders like Terry the Tramp and James Bondo to carry the movement forward. Leaders like Tombstone from the Hessians MC, Junior, the international President of the Sons of Silence, Bandido George, and Jesse from the Outlaws ultimately encouraged their brothers to step up and get involved.

Here are the goals that the Confederation of Clubs put forth:

> *Since the inception of the Confederation of Clubs of Southern California back in 1988, patch holders throughout North America have realized that they have mutual goals that can be achieved by combining their manpower and brainpower. Today, the Confederation of Clubs has become the fastest growing segment of the bikers' rights community, with patch holders forming or in the process of organizing 55 Confederations in 35 States and three Canadian Provinces. Their unifying focus is to fight biker discrimination through the courts and the legislatures. All Confederations are members of the*

National Coalition of Motorcyclists (NCOM) and support their state legislative motorcyclists' rights organizations. A.I.M. Attorneys serve as Legal Counsel. Confederations of Clubs in various states have successfully fought "No Bikers Allowed" and "No Colors" signs in restaurants, bars, and hotels/motels; stopped harassment by specific law enforcement agencies or agents; lobbied for passage of biker anti-discrimination legislation; fought helmet tickets and assisted in the fight against mandatory helmet laws; as well as put together charity runs to raise money and gifts for the needy.

In 2007, Terry the Tramp was awarded a plaque for his efforts with the Confederation. It read:

Terry 'The Tramp' Orendorff is hereby awarded this plaque of appreciation, for being a dedicated and tenacious pioneer in the development of the first Confederation of Clubs, thus starting the legal rights movement for patch holders.

Whereas your tenacious dedication and continual support of our legal rights.

Whereas your outstanding leadership, continual effort and support in our fight to preserve our lifestyle.

Whereas your vision as a pioneer in bringing patch holders together, a tribute to us all, and this accomplishment is of great value to the entire motorcycle community.

—*Richard Lester*

Terry and the Vagos entered a new era, with expanded resources and knowledge, but the treachery didn't subside. Through the Confederation of Clubs, their awareness and knowledge were heightened.

Times were changing. ☠

More Expansion

AS THE CLUB SETTLED IN, ITS PAST CONTINUED to haunt the members. The wild times were still fresh on the authorities' devious, budget-conscious minds. Even so, club members never lost confidence as they roared into the new millennium aboard faster, more reliable choppers. The outlaw clubs were refined from pure motorcycle maniacs on choppers to organized, experienced, and legally savvy groups of hard-riding patriots, searching for freedom, brotherhood, and a rough-and-tumble reputation. Competitive growth became a factor not only in southern California, but internationally as club charters began to expand around the globe.

The Vagos were as interested in expansion as any other club, but only if that expansion didn't come at the expense of others. "I wanted to build the largest club in the world without hurting anyone," Terry said.

Boss was a member of the Vietnam Vets MC when 9/11 hit. He worked at the New York site as a clean-up construction boss, then became a Vago.

> Crime became less a lifestyle and more about choice. Terry chose not to pursue that avenue.

There was also a growing, strident, individual survival aspect. Crime became less a lifestyle and more about choice. Terry chose not to pursue that avenue, but if crime wasn't a vocation for the club, something had to pay the bills. Real jobs, bike shop ownership, various entrepreneurial efforts, product lines, and sales of club paraphernalia became ways to generate income. Club events were another solid source of income in addition to chapter expansion.

Clubs like the Hells Angels expanded into Europe. Initially, the sense of expansion was competitive, even progressive and sexy, but the actual process was daunting. Different states countered with diverse law enforcement practices and techniques, and the states themselves had different outlaw styles. Club guys in Southern California and Detroit were two different breeds, and so were the cops. Clubs in Canada and in Europe used explosives and rocket launchers, not fists, guns, and knives.

Terry began to travel to Hawaii each year to take breaks from the harried day-to-day blitz of troubleshooting, dodging legal arrows in Southern California, negotiating the treacherous waters of intra- and interclub politics, and generally surviving the West Coast hub of club rivalries and tensions. After a couple of years of building relationships with club guys on the islands, Steve Vandal from the Jokers MC approached Terry about initiating a Vago chapter on Maui. Terry instructed Steve in what he believed was the correct manner to establish a chapter. Steve was directed to approach the council of island clubs for consent.

"I didn't want to step into any area and take over," Terry said. "We wanted the respect of the other clubs. We wouldn't back down to anyone, but we would be straight-up about our intentions."

He also asked Steve to fly to California and attend a Confederation of Clubs meeting.

"We didn't want to be a bully club," Terry said, "We also attempted to deal with our own when a member ran into a problem. We tried not to drag the club into personal business."

As the club grew with chapters in Bakersfield, Hemet, Hawaii, Utah, and Nomads in Japan, the authorities couldn't get over the past, and they sought out snitches to infiltrate the club wherever possible. In 1997, informants tipped authorities off to plans from inside the 200-member Vagos club's growing ranks. Because the enforcement world couldn't arrest a club for growing, they needed to demonstrate expanding operations into criminal activities throughout the southwestern U.S. They made every charge appear as devastating as possible.

In each case, the snitch told the authorities as much bullshit as he did club members.

In October 1998, federal and state agents arrested thirteen members in San Fernando Valley, Las Vegas, and San Diego. They were charged with various crimes, including possessing stolen explosives, illegal firearms, and large amounts of methamphetamine and the ingredients to cook it. All arrests were coupled to snitches and agent infiltrators.

In each case the snitch told the authorities as much bullshit as he did club members. The federal Bureau of Alcohol, Tobacco, and Firearms spearheaded arrests from the two-year investigation. In addition to the October 28 bust, in May five more Vagos members were charged with robbery, kidnapping, drug possession, and weapons offenses, according to ATF Special Agent John D'Angelo.

"It was another nothing bust," Terry said. "They busted Vinnie for selling a couple of muscle relaxers to an agent."

"The explosives—about forty pounds of commercial blasting agents believed stolen from a construction site in the Imperial Valley—were found hidden in a house just outside of San Diego," D'Angelo said. "About sixty machine guns, sawed-off shotguns, and rifles were also found in the house."

According to D'Angelo, three men in the house also had in their possession about five pounds of methamphetamine and 100 pounds of ingredients used to make the drug, sold to them by undercover federal agents. They were charged with a variety of drug and weapons crimes.

More members from San Fernando, Reseda, and Northridge were charged with illegally possessing firearms. ATF agents went as far as charging members in Las Vegas with kidnapping, torture, extortion, and racketeering. And the U.S. Attorney's office in Los Angeles planned additional weapons-related arrests in the San Fernando Valley.

"The scope and nature of the charges and the gun seizures speak volumes about the nature of the gang," said ATF Special Agent Richard Carr. "Hopefully, our work will have a lasting and debilitating effect on them."

D'Angelo said it was unclear what plans the gang had for the explosives and weapons in San Diego.

"It's not uncommon with these types of organizations where they find they need to arm themselves in such a way for protection," he said.

Into that atmosphere jumped three undercover federal agents whose mission was to document crimes committed by Vagos gang members in the Los Angeles area.

Posing as hang-arounds, the agents became prospective members. The agents were required to join members at parties and meetings, while they hoped to become initiated into the club. As part of the initiation, they had to purchase beer, work as body-guards at parties, and guard members' motorcycles while they met with members from other states.

Two agents were eventually turned down for membership after they filled out their applications, which were carefully scrutinized. The club was learning. Security checks were handled through a private investigator.

"Cops are generally weak," Terry said, "or their applications point out inconsistencies in their stories."

According to D'Angelo, the Vagos did not feel comfortable with informants, but didn't elaborate any further. He said that the

Terry traveled to Hawaii annually and oversaw new chapters expanding onto the islands. This photo was taken during the 2000 Tramp Birthday dinner. Big C, left, Steve, Sockatese, and Story Teller.

members were very organized about backgrounding people and that the ATF had pulled the agents out for their own safety.

One agent did become a member. "He only lasted a minute," Terry said. "There's a world of difference between a prospect and a member."

The law enforcement heat was turned on high as authorities suspected the worst from the spreading Vagos organization, led by Terry the Tramp. The paranoid government stepped up efforts to bust anything green that moved.

The old adage, "If you do the crime, ya gotta be prepared to do the time," surfaced over and over. But some riders weren't prepared to do the time. In August 2001, a law enforcement task force raided Vago homes and businesses in the Antelope and San Fernando Valleys, arresting twenty-three suspects in an alleged methamphetamine ring. The *Los Angeles Times* reported that the group had links to white supremacy groups and Mexican drug suppliers.

A predawn raid culminated the eighteen-month Operation Silent Thunder operation, targeting Antelope Valley methamphetamine

The army of more than 200 officers and agents from the FBI, Los Angeles Sheriffs, Drug Enforcement Administration, the State Department of Corrections, and the Los Angeles Police hit 21 sites in Lancaster, Leona Valley, Chatsworth, and Palmdale at 4:00 a.m.

cookers and dealers. The sweep operation netted 293 arrests and scored $500,000 in cash and more than forty-five pounds of meth with an estimated street value of $2 million.

During those hot summer raids, officers confiscated 125 weapons, including a grenade launcher, AK-47 assault rifles, semiautomatic rifles with bayonets, and explosives. Cars, trucks, motorcycles, motorized water skis, knives with Nazi emblems, and other Nazi paraphernalia were seized.

The cops made a big deal of the score on national television during a news conference, where Sheriff Lee Baca displayed the weapons cache. He proudly pointed out that his operation dismantled a meth network extending throughout the western United States.

The army of more than 200 officers and agents from the FBI, Los Angeles Sheriffs, Drug Enforcement Administration, the State Department of Corrections, and the Los Angeles Police hit twenty-one sites in Lancaster, Leona Valley, Chatsworth, and Palmdale at 4:00 a.m.

"The high desert should not be a place where known criminals can come and think they can prosper," Baca said.

Officials said the purity of the seized methamphetamine ranged from 83 percent to 97 percent, powerful portions of the highly addictive drug. The operation also shut down sixteen meth labs, sheriff's officials said. Reports published in the newspaper consisted predominately of bullshit assertions and allegations.

"They are career criminals, including many associated with organizations practicing white supremacist ideologies," said Margarita Velazquez, a Sheriff's Department spokeswoman.

Of the 293 suspects arrested during the entire investigation, authorities said 233 had criminal records. Nearly 200 were on parole or probation, including one man on probation for attempted murder, and seventy-two were members of white supremacist groups, Baca claimed.

As usual, the costly commando operation netted few convictions, but it did turn two Hemet chapter Vagos into snitches. One member busted with the forty-five pounds of meth turned, and would return to haunt the club through another law enforcement operation. Another member, Big Roy, was busted for selling a gun as a felon.

"His attorney recommended that he take the plea," said Terry. "He took the deal, went to jail, then they discovered the weapon was actually a paint gun. Too late."

The new millennium meant enhanced drug enforcement, with new laws, new threats, and higher police budgets. With club expansion came heightened enforcement and less control for Terry. It was one thing to be the boss of a handful of charters around Southern California, but charters around the globe were not as malleable. Paranoid law enforcement ran out of control, and another evil spirit loomed. Greed within the club festered like infected road rash on an injured elbow. Terry's toughest decade was yet to come. ☠

It's Easy to Start a War

DRUGS AND WOMEN START WARS BETWEEN CLUBS," Terry said. "I tried to keep the club name good, but drugs got in the way, and every time they came into play there were problems."

Tension peaked whenever rival clubs were thrust into the same venue. In 2001, a fight broke out in an Orange County Fairgrounds swap meet. The melee started at 8:15 in the evening when the wrong Hells Angels came in contact with members of the Vagos.

"As combatants grabbed merchandise off vendors' tables and began hitting each other, others joined the brawl, which soon involved

The Dirty Dozen was for decades the only one percenter club in Arizona. Times have changed, and in the 1980s, the Vagos established a charter in Lake Havasu. Gary, the gun dealer, was an upstanding Vago member of the Havasu Charter.

dozens more people," reported Jessica Garrison in her *Los Angeles Times* article.

Two elements came into play on that overcast Southern California day. During the 1980s, intimidation was a key factor within the club world. A straight citizen who rode a motorcycle wasn't safe around a group of one-percenters. That left a large population of citizens out in the cold. Many held grudges, fear, and distrust for club guys, while others tried to align themselves with a club they believed would stand up to a bully club. The crowd was split at the Orange County fairgrounds under the pre-fab roof and bright fluorescent lights.

The melee started at 8:15 in the evening when the wrong Hells Angels came in contact with members of the Vagos.

Jon Erickson attended the swap meet to help a friend who was a vendor. "There was a fight between Vagos and Hells Angels, between everybody, dude. I saw a lot of people getting hit with handlebars, gas tanks. There was blood everywhere."

His friend, Eric Maurer, said he was at his booth when he heard a commotion. "Then I saw a crowd of four people expand exponentially. There were sixty or seventy people in the melee. I saw people getting hit around the head with steel bars. One man got hit square in the center of his skull. I heard it hit his head; then his head went 'Whack!' on the cement deck."

After just five minutes, the fight broke up, Maurer said, and there was a headlong rush for the exits. Dozens of officers from the Costa Mesa, Irvine, Huntington Beach, and Newport Beach police departments responded, along with Orange County Sheriff's Department personnel and several ambulances and fire engines. Authorities closed the swap meet and police officers in helmets and facemasks stood in formation around the perimeter.

Sheriff's Lt. Dennis DeMaio said a man was arrested on suspicion of assaulting a police officer. His name was not released. Vendors waited anxiously to reclaim their merchandise, abandoned in the guarded structure while police cleared the area. Sheriff's officials said two injured people were treated at the scene and released.

"It's easy to start a war," Terry said, "but they're a bitch to stop, especially if someone dies in the conflict."

The Confederation of Clubs afforded clubs the opportunity to discuss issues in a neutral zone. It also afforded them a venue to share their renegade experiences. They rapidly saw that all club brothers faced similar issues, under similar circumstances. The Confederation created a calming effect.

Unfortunately, expansion pushed the notion of all brothers getting along in a different, acrimonious direction. Another drawback to expansion was cocked and loaded into a large-caliber weapon of conflict. Two clubs could commingle in California, but split skulls on the East Coast.

Steve, from the Jokers in Hawaii, became the boss of the Hawaiian Vagos. In 2004, he lost a leg in an island motorcycle accident. Terry flew to Hawaii and spent days beside Steve's hospital bed. Steve was never the same.

"He became bitter," Terry said. "When he lost his leg, he lost his heart."

While Terry met with potential members in Utah, Oregon, and Nevada, not all new charters survived.

"We tried in North Carolina," Terry said, "But I was forced to fly out and bring all the patches back."

Some charters grew and flourished; others stumbled and fell.

"I had to make it clear that once they had a charter, they had to manage all aspects," Terry said. "I couldn't fly out every time someone skinned a knee."

Some brothers became charter missionaries. There was Rattles in Utah, and C.J., who set up Vegas, Carson City, and Reno. And Spike helped form additional chapters in Southern California.

"Spike set up the South Side Chapter," Terry said. "He helped keep some faltering charters together. He was good at dealing with internal club politics and other clubs."

"It's easy to start a war," Terry said, "but they're a bitch to stop, especially if someone dies in the conflict."

The club became more powerful and nationally recognized, and Terry was at the top of the rock. "So lots of folks shot arrows at me," he said.

While chapters grew, the feds desperately worked with snitches to bring down the Vago organization. Federal and state authorities concluded a two-year investigation in 2002, when they arrested twelve members in four counties on suspicion of drug and weapons charges.

A dozen members were arrested out of more than 200 in Southern California. The investigation was wrapped around a snitch member of the Vagos named Hammer. He was six-foot one-inch tall, with short black hair and a Fu Manchu mustache.

"He was charismatic and well-liked," Terry said of the snitch, "but he was a straight rat."

> The club became more powerful and nationally recognized, and Terry was at the top of the rock. "So lots of folks shot arrows at me," he said.

Hammer was busted in Redondo Beach for failing to pay a prostitute. He couldn't face the time for the crime and turned on his brothers.

"I noticed that as soon as he was cut loose from his last beef, he flew around the country like a free man," Terry said. "He was supposedly on parole. It didn't add up. I immediately steered clear of him. He started to smell like a rat."

Hammer flew to Hawaii and tried to hang out with the club while sporting a video camera.

"He said it was cool, since he was visiting a cousin," Terry said.

As it turned, out the so-called cousin was his police connection. He tried to purchase weapons on the islands and capture video footage of members at parties.

"I took the camera away from him," Terry said, "and we kicked him off the island."

Hammer secretly cooperated with authorities, and used government money to buy illegal firearms and drugs, according to Jeffrey

Ferguson, an Orange County deputy district attorney. The deputy DA said Hammer provided authorities with unusual insight into the club's plans to traffic methamphetamine and firearms.

Authorities paid Hammer to snitch on his brothers, make up crimes, and glorify minor offenses for his own financial gain.

"He was really tired of going to prison and wanted to get out of the life," Ferguson said.

"That's bullshit," Terry retorted. "He did the crime and didn't have the balls to do the time."

Federal officials obtained grand jury indictments and state criminal complaints against twelve people. Then groups of law enforcement officers fanned out across Los Angeles, Orange, Riverside, and San Bernardino counties on June 18 to serve federal and state arrest warrants on the suspects.

Hammer secretly cooperated with authorities, and used government money to buy illegal firearms and drugs, according to Jeffrey Ferguson, an Orange County deputy district attorney.

"Among those arrested were officers of several Vagos chapters," said Letice Baker, a spokeswoman for the U.S. Bureau of Alcohol, Tobacco, and Firearms. Teams of cops seized eighty-five firearms and an unspecified quantity of narcotics, Baker said. Several agencies were involved, including the state Department of Justice, the ATF, the Orange County district attorney's office, Santa Ana police, and Los Angeles and San Bernardino County Sheriff's Departments.

Officials identified two suspects, Dennis Lee "Bonehead" Watlington, fifty-nine, of Rialto and Richard Garcia Jr., forty-three, of Westminster, both Vagos. They were held at the Orange County Jail on $500,000 bail.

Watlington was charged with conspiring to sell an illegal assault rifle and belonging to a criminal street gang. By this time law enforcement officials had discovered that they could generate hostility toward clubs by calling them gangs, thus associating them with

"That's bullshit," **Terry retorted. "He did the crime and didn't have the balls to do the time."** the ethnic street gangs that came to prominence in urban areas in the 1970s and 1980s and harnessing racist sentiments in the general population to use against members of motorcycle clubs.

The term "gang" itself constitutes sort of a garbage category and has no agreed-upon meaning, even among the most prudent researchers of the topic. Cities, states and countries all have differing views on what constitutes a gang. In 1988 the state of California defined a criminal street gang as any organization, association, or group of three or more persons, whether formal or informal, which (1) has continuity of purpose, (2) seeks a group identity, and (3) has members who individually or collectively engage in or have engaged in a pattern of criminal activity. This awkwardly written, vague, and redundant definition is really more of a non-definition because it offers an extremely simplified view of a gang as being "criminal," regardless of whether or not any crimes are committed. According to this definition, any youth who participates in a gang can be labeled as a "criminal" regardless of their individual activity or role. Prosecutors have been able to exploit the flaw in the definition to their benefit by applying gang-related "enhancements" that can transform a simple misdemeanor offense into a felony that carries heavier penalties, including prison time.

In Watlington's case the state's nonsensical definition of a "criminal gang" had very real consequences; because he was convicted of assaulting a sheriff's deputy in Los Angeles County in 1999, he faced more than twenty years in prison.

"He got seventeen years, because his son testified against him," Terry said. "He was basically tried for being a felon with a gun. Another bullshit charge."

Garcia was accused of selling an automatic weapon and a sawed-off shotgun, Ferguson said.

He faced more than twenty years in prison if convicted, but he got off. It turned into another expensive, hollow case, but the law enforcement community was forced to justify their big-buck budgets, and expanding one-percenter clubs were easy targets.

"I warned everyone about Hammer," Terry said, "but he was considered a good shit within the club."

Hammer took his life with an overdose of drugs after he was moved out of state in the witness protection program.

The more the Vagos grew, the more heat the green machine pulled from all corners of law enforcement. In 2006, after two charters were established in Utah, one in Oregon, two in Nevada, four in Hawaii, and after the nationally recognized club survived three turbulent decades, two snitches from within tried once more to take the Vagos down. This time, 750 law enforcement officials conducted sweeps in five Southern California counties. According to the *LA Times*, they intended to break the Vagos' back.

> **Hammer took his life with an overdose of drugs after he was moved out of state in the witness protection program.**

"It was a case of Rats on Rats," Terry said.

The newspaper reported that the Vagos were established in the 1960s to deal drugs and weapons, which was news to Terry and the other long-time members, but such nonsense sold papers and helped law-enforcement efforts. Some twenty-two bikers were arrested in LA, San Bernardino, Riverside, Ventura, and Orange counties, after three years of investigation using a Hemet chapter member of the Vagos, and Charles, a Victorville member, as informants.

Once more authorities thought they could curtail the Vagos's extensive operations. According to reports from high-paid law enforcement authorities, the counterculture movement was actually a highly sophisticated criminal enterprise with a vast hand in the methamphetamine trade.

"Today is just the beginning," said Orange County Sheriff Michael S. Carona. "The Hells Angels, the Vagos . . . they are not clubs. The reality is that they're supporting terrorism."

According to the *LA Times*, Vagos leaders had long denied having any ties to criminal activity. The Vagos website stated that the group was formed as a "tight brotherhood to survive the wars between the rival clubs and the constant harassment of the police." The Internet message went on to say, "Vagos comes from the Spanish language meaning 'traveling gypsy' or 'a streetwise person that's always up to something.'"

By 2006, the Vagos membership swelled to more than 300 members in California, Arizona, Nevada, Hawaii, and Mexico.

> In post-9/11 America, a period during which the country effectively lost its collective mind and saw terrorists hiding behind every shrub, it was only a matter of time before law enforcement began exploiting the fear of terrorism in its persecution of clubs like the Vagos.

Law enforcement boasted that the Vagos investigation was among the largest coordinated law enforcement probes ever conducted in the region. They arrested seven chapter presidents, one vice president, one secretary, one treasurer, and seven sergeants-at-arms. Officials said they seized ninety-five illegal firearms, various illegal drugs including methamphetamine, $6,000 in cash, and two stolen motorcycles. And of course, they threatened to turn the investigation into a federal racketeering case. It was incredible, the level of bullshit and legalese promulgated against a bunch of hard-riding bikers. Their bandolier of legal ammunition grew as racketeering (RICO) and street gang laws were used to curtail club growth.

Since the 1980s many states had adopted legislation and laws specifically drafted to combat street gangs and to make it easier to prosecute their offenses, according to StreetGang.com. California led the nation in laws written to prosecute gangs, but many other states initiated their own laws.

Then after 9/11, terrorism laws were enacted to enhance law enforcement's stranglehold on society. But nothing stopped the

Vagos's growth. In post-9/11 America, a period during which the country effectively lost its collective mind and saw terrorists hiding behind every shrub, it was only a matter of time before law enforcement began exploiting the fear of terrorism in its persecution of clubs like the Vagos. The Homeland Security Act and the establishment of the Department of Homeland Security gave unscrupulous law enforcement agencies an entirely new palette of laws to abuse in this pursuit.

Given the zeal with which law enforcement has pursued the Vagos over the past four decades, and the fact that all these investigations over all these years have only produced a handful of relatively low-level convictions, one has to wonder why the establishment is so threatened by clubs like the Vagos. German philosopher Max Weber might have provided an answer to that. Weber defined a nation state as an entity that maintained and exercised a monopoly on violence. In other words, power resides in the hands of those with the authority to hurt and kill, that is, those who control an army. In the United States that army takes the form of law enforcement agencies.

Clubs like the Hells Angels, the Vagos, and the Bandidos represent a direct threat to the state's monopoly on the use of violence because they are, in many ways, organized armies not controlled by the state. Thus they are a threat to the state, whether they are cooking meth and running prostitution operations or giving blood and hosting toy runs. The threat from a motorcycle club is not the club's criminal activity; the threat from a motorcycle club is the club's very existence. Because of this, the state will hound a motorcycle club relentlessly, even if the only crimes committed are committed by the state itself in the act of persecuting the club.

This is not to say that all clubs, including the Vagos, are composed of saintly choir boys, because they're not. Rather, the point is that it doesn't really matter what a club does because the state perceives a motorcycle club as a threat just because it exists. If clubs are growing, the perceived threat is growing. And in the early 2000s, the Vagos was a growing club. "The more we grew, the more bullets I had to dodge," Terry said.

Terry's notorious stepbrother, Eddie, a.k.a. Parts. Parts was as tough as they come, but finally succumbed to cancer and died in 2006. He always had Terry's back.

The club might have been growing, but the circle of people Terry could trust was shrinking. Perhaps the biggest loss was the death of his stepbrother Parts, who died of cancer in 2006. Parts was the true gangster in the family. He fought anyone and everyone, dealt drugs, moved stolen goods, and abused women.

"He didn't take shit from anyone," Terry said. "He'd listen for a minute, but when you thought it was time for a fight, he was already throwing punches."

The man had many character flaws, but there was a straight-up aspect to Parts's personality. He was true and honest. He didn't fight without reason or provocation. He was pure Vago and never backed down from anyone. All the clubs respected him.

"He was my closest brother while I was in prison," Silver said.

He ate women up and spit them out. "I never understood it," Terry said. "He

> **Parts was the true gangster in the family. He fought anyone and everyone, dealt drugs, moved stolen goods, and abused women.**

would smack one around and she'd come crawling back." A broad magnet, he was a good-looking, longhaired, swaggering brunette biker. He always had four or five strippers working for him, bringing home the tips.

"Parts was the first Vago I ever met," Silver said. "He embodied the Vagos and got me into the club under age. He was laid back, but had an explosive temper. I never saw him drunk or loaded."

Terry and Eddie, or Parts, were the same height, but Parts was thinner, yet he was still stocky. He worked out with weights constantly. But at sixty the big C hit him in the lungs, even though he had quit smoking five years earlier and never had smoked as much as Terry. Cancer was the first and only nemesis to kick his ass. It riddled him quickly and he spent the last week of his life at Terry's home. He wasted away.

"He was a proud man," Silver said. "He had the best-looking women, so when he started to fade, he didn't want to see anyone."

One of his real sisters, Dorothy, ran rest homes, and offered to help, so Terry hauled his dying brother back to his Lake Havasu home to meet his RN sister for his final days. He ran at life hard until the end, and then death came without warning and kicked his ass.

The 2006 law enforcement operation was dubbed "22-Green," because Vagos gang members wore the number 22 on their vests, representing V, the 22nd letter of the alphabet, and green was the gang's color.

In an effort to justify the investigation, authorities alleged that the Vagos gang also had a long history of involvement in the manufacture and distribution of methamphetamine, as well as other controlled substances. They were believed to be responsible for selling drugs in parks in San Bernardino County, officials said.

Because the Vagos were classified as a criminal street gang, judges could add enhanced penalties if members were convicted.

Because the Vagos were classified as a criminal street gang, judges could add enhanced penalties if members were convicted.

Among those whose homes were searched that notorious Thursday was Terry the Tramp's residence in the high desert town of Hesperia. Although he was not arrested, Terry and other club leaders remained subject to future federal racketeering charges, based on the gang's alleged involvement in a July 2004 killing in Lucerne Valley and an attempted murder in Hesperia, authorities said.

Those arrested included chapter presidents Scott "Psycho" Sikoff of Apple Valley, Vincent Mariano of Victorville, Nels "Swede" Bloom of Romoland, "Big" Roy Compton III of San Jacinto, Lino "Umpire" Garcia of Oxnard, and sergeant at arms Michael "Chainsaw" Izykowski of Huntington Beach.

"We expect some of the gang leadership to cooperate with us," said Thomas Mangan, spokesman for the Bureau of Alcohol, Tobacco, Firearms and Explosives. "This is the just the tip of the iceberg."

As usual, a bunch of members were arrested, but only a couple of Vagos were actually convicted. Still, the war between the Man and the Vagos raged on. What once were fist-fighting, beer-chugging bikers became high-crime, street terrorists running vast drug networks, according to authorities begging the government for more funds, enlarged staffs, and more control. Terry was in the middle of the fracas, between clubs champing at the bit to battle it out and law enforcement agencies grappling for any excuse to enact tougher penalties, build larger prisons, hire vast networks of agents, and expand their powers.

Terry had quit drinking, but he chain-smoked and drank coffee like a man on death row. His hair thinned but his dedication to the club never faltered. He would do anything to prevent a war or allow drugs to pull the Vagos down. Yet as the club grew, so did factions within the organization, factions that didn't have Terry's best interests at heart. Most men were afraid of the fireplug with the dead-straight gaze. He melted most men's bravado, and set any bullshit story straight. ☠

Desert Delights and Pitfalls

TERRY AND THE VAGOS RIPPED THROUGH the first five years of the new millennium like their tires were on fire. Terry tried to keep drug dealing away from the club, but many brothers wrapped themselves in the outlaw lifestyle with meth dealing, marijuana, and coke. Most one-percenter organizations banned opiates, and some forced addicted members to the streets. Terry gave no quarter for drug dealing, especially around his own home.

"I met a girl who had recently left her husband," Terry said. "I got her a place to live and co-signed for a car." Lilly was a hot, five-foot seven-inch cowgirl on the weekends and all business during the week. "She had bright blue eyes and long, straight, jet-black hair," Terry said, "always fixed it just right."

Terry came home to his little string of lath-and-plaster cottages in El Monte one night to find Lilly with an ex. "I was cool with who-ever came around, but he wanted to leave three pounds of speed in her unit, and I wasn't having it."

The guy said it was only for a quick hour and persisted. "I said that hour could cost me twenty years," Terry said, and told him to take his shit and leave.

An ex-member who was kicked out for being hooked on drugs. Note the bottom rocker. Shortly after this photo was taken in 1999, the Vagos switched to California bottom rockers, once an exclusive with the Hells Angels in California.

Lilly went ballistic. She was a bright star in public and a bitch in private. Terry moved to be nearer to her in Victorville in 2000, but the run from his shop in Los Angeles to the desert was daunting.

The notion to move to no-man's land on the edge of the Mojave Desert was alluring. He owned eight dogs and the thought of an acre of open land away from the city, the cops, and the bullshit enticed him away from the city and the heart of the Vago empire.

From a club-politics prospective, the move was not in his best interests. His new, single-story ranch home behind the town of Hesperia sat back off Sultana road, behind privacy-coated chain-link fence in the blistering desert sun. He shut his shop down, escaped Lilly's wrath, and started to date the real estate agent who sold him his desert hideout.

Janet, also from Hesperia and recently divorced, owned a crane company, and ran a real estate brokerage. She was sharp as a new Gillette razor blade, and that precision edge came with a dangerous allure. As Terry escaped the constant, day-to-day one-percenter turmoil in the asphalt jungle of 12 million for the rural suburbs, he hoped the brothers in green had his back. He had been at the helm since 1986, and his confidence grew with each legal run-in, with charter expansion, and with the confidence-building vote by the officers to make him IP forever. Plus stepping back from the front line allowed any anti-Tramp faction to fester, like mold on a ripening peach.

> There was no end to the vagabond treachery, or the conniving police lurking behind long-distance lenses and sound-amplifying devices, attempting to capture the green renegades spreading around the southland.

There was no end to the vagabond treachery, or the conniving police lurking behind long-distance lenses and sound-amplifying devices, attempting to capture the green renegades spreading around the southland. Authorities tried to pin murder on the Vagos when a Lytle Creek man disappeared. When investigators searched the home of John Edward Rintalan, fifty-four, they discovered a considerable amount of human blood. Three weeks after Rintalan was reported missing, on April 3, 2007, his body was discovered, dumped on a roadway near Phelan, California, just down a shrubbery-covered bluff from the home of a Vago. Officials believed the murder was connected to the gang.

"In reality," Terry said, "It was another trumped-up charge against the Vagos. The rumor was that the chick shot her landlord. According the the newspaper reports, she shot the guy and thought she killed him." Apparently they'd wrapped him with duct-tape and dumped the man, still alive, in a ditch. "He suffocated."

Federal agents arrested John "Pelone" Loza, fifty-eight, after being tipped off. He worked in a traveling carnival and his wife, Jeanne, was picked up in Lake Havasu, Arizona.

Terry dodged most bullets, although a real one still resided near his spine. He splintered most political arrows, but a new twist emerged. Could he dodge every indictment, every political scheme? His home on the edge of the desert was still his son's residence, along with a couple of other loyal brothers. The single-story, white, ranch-style home with the tile roof was clean. The interior was simply adorned, with western paintings, Vagos memorabilia, and John Wayne prints. A calendar of black-and-white John Wayne movie stills was tacked to the stucco wall above the kitchen telephone. A chunk of burlwood hung in the dining room with a tribute to his brother Parts resined to the thick grain.

Terry and the Duke were similar in many respects. They were hard-riding, hard-fighting, no-bullshit sonsabitches. They didn't pull punches with fists or words. Like Wayne, Terry was boot-tough and rattlesnake-mean.

Over the years, after experiencing numerous searches by various law enforcement agencies, Terry learned not to keep any Vagos artifacts, clippings, or photographs near his home. During his thirty years as a member and a leader, he had no warrants and no convictions, yet the law was constantly after his ass, viewing him as the evil perpetrator of anything green that screamed through the night to raise hell on a glistening chopper. He didn't even drink, except for a constantly steaming cup of coffee, which kept him brewing like boiling oil.

Terry was about to face several final challenges. Had he rolled the green dice too many times, trusted the wrong brothers, and pounded his chest too hard in front of the wrong factions? Or were times changing, and younger guns reaching for the green reigns? Would he become a Vago scapegoat, a target once again, or the prey of evil club factions?

Hemet, California, a sleepy little town at the foot of the mountains leading to San Jacinto and Idyllwild, is a touristy, low-elevation mountain community, home to hippies and tree huggers. Hemet was founded in 1887 and quickly became a retirement community just fifty miles southeast of the Los Angeles City squalor. But as the first decade of the new century closed in 2010, it became the next city to attack the Vagos, after four city code-enforcement trucks were burned to the ground in the parking lot of the Hemet City Hall.

"Hemet was never good to Vagos," Terry said.

Officials immediately suspected the growing green machine in their town. There had been three additional attacks on the Hemet-San Jacinto Gang Task Force before December, 2010. During the first surreptitious strike, someone scaled the roof of the undercover gang headquarters and redirected an open natural gas pipeline inside, filling the building with fumes. A single spark would have leveled the building with a massive explosion. In February, a homemade zip gun was planted in the iron gate of the task force parking lot. It was set to go off when the gate was opened, and when it did, it just missed a gang task force officer. Next an officer discovered a dangerous device affixed to his unmarked vehicle. A local gang was retaliating because of an enforcement sweep. Then an anonymous caller dialed 911 and threatened an attack on a police car in two days if the investigation was not halted.

"We are assuming, because of the timing, that this is related to the other three attacks on our gang task force," said Lt. Duane Wisehart, who was filmed standing near the charred crime scene off of busy Florida Avenue, just two blocks from the Hemet Police Station. "We are looking mostly at gangs as suspects, because our task force is being targeted."

Somebody torched the truck engines around 11:30 p.m. A man spotted nearby was questioned and released. Detectives quickly reviewed video surveillance camera tapes.

"Every day, we worry about what's next," Wisehart said.

Attorney General Jerry Brown visited the Hemet area with Riverside County District Attorney Rod Pacheco and offered a $200,000 reward for the capture of the culprits. Brown called it, "urban terrorism."

The day before Brown's visit, officials in Riverside County, Utah, Arizona, and Nevada launched a massive crackdown on the Vagos, which had a chapter in Hemet and a supposed history of violence toward police. They arrested thirty members from Riverside County on drug and weapons charges.

Pacheco painted the Vagos as a 2,000-strong, evil gang, and said the sleepy town of Hemet was "Ground Zero."

Hemet police chief Richard Dana was afraid to let his team investigate the crime scene during the twilight hours. "I wasn't going to leave my men out there alone," he said. "Maybe this was an attempt to get them out in the open and attack again."

Down the street from the crime scene, new barricades and barbed wire were strung around the gang task-force facility. The city of Hemet quickly spent an additional $155,000 on barricades and fences. It took on the appearance of a fortress. The ATF and FBI were called to investigate, along with explosive-sniffing dogs.

The next day, blast-proof glass was installed in the Hemet Police Department windows, and roadblocks were set up around the facility. Officers monitored surveillance cameras 24/7. Overnight, Hemet became a war zone.

For more than five decades, Hemet had been considered a sleepy retirement community. Dairy cows roamed vast, rolling fields. Gradually large sprawling farms and ranch homes surrounded by stately

Hemet police chief Richard Dana was afraid to let his team investigate the crime scene during the twilight hours.

pepper and oak shade trees were mowed down to make way for cookie-cutter, stucco tract homes and lackluster strip malls. Young families, looking to escape the city and live cheaply, flocked to the base of the San Jacinto Mountains. But members from 100 different clubs and gangs from Los Angeles and Moreno Valley also moved into Hemet.

One month local law enforcement arrested thirty-three Vagos in their paranoid move to find the perpetrators of the attacks against their gang task force. The next month they arrested another twenty-three, searched thirty-five locations in the vicinity, and seized sixteen weapons. Riverside County District Attorney Rod Pacheco said in an interview that the Vagos were "an extreme threat to law enforcement."

During one of these Hemet-related raids in Desert Hot Springs, a SWAT team raided a dentist's office during working hours. "The office was full of patients when they stormed in," Terry said. The dentist was a member of the Vagos, and he immediately sued the agency behind the raid.

A week after the crackdown against club members, less than half of the members arrested had been formally charged. Joseph Yanny, a Vagos attorney from Beverly Hills, told the *LA Times* that none of the folks arrested were Vagos.

"As far as I'm concerned, this is nothing but politics," Yanny said. "They know none of the people arrested were guilty of anything."

The same story ran four times in the *Los Angeles Times*, with the same accusations against the Vagos regarding the same low-brow attacks against the Gang Task Force. It was as if the media and city officials were on a witch hunt, or were trying to drum up support for a larger police presence, because they had no clue as to who the actual attackers were.

Hemet city officials turned up the heat on the Vagos. They genuinely believed that the club was out to kill them and they lived in abject fear for their lives. Experts and the media exploited the minor attacks, hyperbolizing them into a study of white supremacists with shaved heads, tattoos, combat boots, and fatigues moving into the fertile ground around Hemet.

"There is a significant concentration of hate groups in the Inland

Empire, unlike anywhere else in the nation, from the National Socialist Movement to the Hammerskins to the Comrades of our Racist Struggle," said Brian Levin, the director of the Center for the Study of Hate and Extremism at Cal State San Bernardino. Hemet city authorities were so afraid, they would only speak to the press anonymously.

The paranoid delusions the officials had regarding the Vagos couldn't have been more misplaced. The Vagos might have behaved in ways that would generate legitimate complaints at times, but they were not a hate group. The Vagos didn't hate anyone. They just hated being fucked with.

Hemet arrested two men in connection with the war on local authorities. As it turned out, Nicholas John Smitt, forty, of Hemet, was pissed for being busted for cultivating marijuana, and turned on the cops. Smitt had nothing to do with gangs or motorcycle clubs; he was simply a dope smoker who didn't like his crop of weed being fucked with.

They also arrested Steven Hansen, thirty-six, a convicted arsonist, in nearby Homeland. He was taken into custody on a parole violation for weapons possession, but he wasn't booked on any connection to the police department attacks.

"The community is relieved," said Hemet Mayor Eric McBride. "They wanted to see closure on this, and now we have some progress."

After arresting more than fifty gang-related affiliates for nothing, after smashing doors down and harassing bikers, Hemet authorities discovered that one individual, Smitt, had organized seven attacks, including three arson attacks.

Ultimately, Smitt was charged with nine felonies, including one count of attempted murder for his zip-gun booby trap. He faced numerous life sentences. His buddy, Hansen, was hit with all the arson-related crimes and faced thirty years in prison. Neither one had anything to do with the Vagos. As it turned out, most of Smitt's attacks coincided with his court appearances on the drug charges. DNA evidence collected from a failed rocket attack turned out to be critical evidence leading to the arrests.

Prison Blues

TERRY THE TRAMP WONDERED WHAT WOULD HAPPEN NEXT. It was another time of change within the Vago structure. With Terry sequestered in the high desert on the outskirts of Hesperia, separated both physically and spiritually from day-to-day club activities, political factions festered and grew within the club ranks. New members wanted to imprint their style on the club. As the guaranteed lifelong international president, Terry stood directly in their path. Shifting dynamics flew at Terry like double-aught buckshot from a shotgun.

Deep inside, the Tramp's psyche was tough as iron. He wanted life to run his way, or be sent down the highway. But without his iron fist enforcing his will at every club function, he no longer held the spark he once did. Suddenly he faced daunting challenges. His

Big Rick was busted in 2006 on a bullshit weapons charge. He went to prison in Lompoc and was assigned to mentor Terry when he arrived in 2010.

With Terry sequestered in the high desert on the outskirts of Hesperia, separated both physically and spiritually from day-to-day club activities, political factions festered and grew within club ranks.

leadership role changed with his relocation 75 miles from the heart of the Vago Nation, yet he initially expected total control from a distance.

All this began to come to a head right around the time Parts was dying. His lifelong friend, sister, and wife, Pam, had died in a car accident. If that wasn't enough to deal with, one day his attorney called regarding an old 2001 federal court case for tax evasion. It was serious; Terry could face jail time.

Throughout Terry's history with the club, through a quarter century of positive, unblinking leadership, he commanded immense respect from his club brothers. But the club was changing, and the old battleship's admiral wouldn't budge from his chain-hardened dock. The more he pounded his Formica counter, the fewer brothers rode way into the desert to listen.

"Terry had fifty leading brothers behind him," Spike said, "but he wouldn't budge on some issues."

For the first time in Terry's outlaw life, he also faced serious jail time, which also added to leader's disconnect from the changing club infrastructure. When the cat's away, the mice will run amok.

"It was just a time of change," Terry admitted, but he had a tough time accepting a new leadership forum, which drove even more brothers away from him.

Maybe they were justified; maybe not. For the first time in his life as a leader, Terry put himself in a vulnerable position. He was no longer at the helm of the green battleship, waiting each night on the outlaw bridge for members to check in with him at Denny's or Sambo's. He relied on loyal brothers in the city to be his eyes, ears, mouth, and fists as he took refuge in his pastoral sanctuary, feeding his pack of eight dogs on the edge of the Mojave Desert.

Plus it looked like Terry could be serving a court-ordered jail stretch because of the federal charge. If Terry was removed from the streets, even for a few months, the current leadership would find itself free to weave its political spell and guide the green machine in their chosen direction, good or bad.

Terry had no resources except for professed brotherhood; he had no defenses against the power struggle being played out within the Vagos' political elite. Thinking he was on firm ground, Terry pushed back against the forces conspiring against him, but like the Duke— John Wayne—sometimes did, Terry pushed too hard.

Meanwhile, Terry waited for his tax evasion hearing to determine his sentence. During this time his income stream dried up. For years he controlled the club purse strings, but because he was headed for jail time he relinquished the club accounts. Part of the tactic taken by those conspiring against him involved implications of financial impropriety—rumors flew around that he had club money—and blaming him for the club's financial troubles so he was unable to turn to the club for any monetary backup.

"I was told trusted brothers had my back," Terry said.

This turned out to be the darkest period of Terry's life. His brother had died, his health was failing, he'd lost control of the club that had been his life for decades, and he lacked even the funds to pay his tax fine and faced doing jail time on account of it. He didn't have a spare dime.

But nothing was as clear-cut as it seemed. When the club voted to make Terry the lifelong international president, for a brief moment it seemed that things were turning Terry's way. But the seeming victory was short-lived.

For the first time in his life, the sixty-three-year-old Terry the Tramp was destined to stand in front of a judge for a sentencing hearing to decide his fate. Terry had other things to worry about, too. One of his close brothers, J.J., was dying of cancer. One morn- ing while Terry awaited sentencing, he made another pot of Folgers coffee and thought about J.J., who had remained a Vago for more than thirty-five years, always a member of the San Gabriel Valley Chapter. A chapter president for a decade, J.J. rode constantly. Terry remembered how a bison once punctured J.J.'s lung while riding in Azusa Canyon.

"He broke his leg so many times," Terry said, "he always rode with a crutch. One bad leg always hung out in the wind."

One night at the famous El Monte Denny's, J.J. went down in the oily parking lot.

"Terry, straighten my leg," J.J. hollered from the pavement.

His leg was twisted and mangled in leather chaps. Terry called for a prospect to help. Later that night, with a cast on his leg, he returned to ride with his brothers, flying his colors on his denim cut.

> He sold motorcycles, gave up a Hollywood studio career, and sold homes to bail brothers out.

Terry pondered the support he had given J.J. and all his other brothers. He thought about the substantial defense funds he arranged for other members. He sold motorcycles, gave up a Hollywood studio career, and sold homes to bail brothers out. He coordinated defense strategies, arranged for witnesses, and defended brothers with everything he had. He left the mother of his child and the love of his life for the club. Now he stood in front of a judge on a low-buck tax-evasion charge. Terry was nearly broke.

On the day he finally was sentenced, he wasn't completely alone. Billy, one remaining loyal club brother, stood by his side. He didn't know what the club was up to, and the club didn't know what Terry faced in the Los Angeles Federal Court when the judge slammed his gavel down.

"Ninety days," the judge ordered, and closed his file on Terry the Tramp. Just ninety days in a minimum-security facility in Lompoc, California. He also faced an additional three years of probation and a $48,000 fine.

Terry relied on his trusted friend, John, and his son, Terry the Wall, to ensure his home would remain upright during his

Mule (left) and Sweetbaby Possum (right) from the Victorville charter in 2006. Possum died in Lompoc, California, of a massive heart attack.

short prison term. He was forced to sell tools and vehicles to cover his mortgage.

To make matters worse, health problems that Terry had been having since the mid-1990s began to get worse. Terry experienced his first heart attack at the age of forty-seven while he was having his way with a beautiful blonde in her second-story Hacienda Heights apartment.

"She kicked my ass," Terry said. "I rolled over and couldn't breathe."

They called 911 and an ambulance hauled Terry's heart-attacked ass to the hospital, but Terry didn't take well to confinement in a hospital bed; the next day he was back at his office at Denny's. One day the bubbly blonde who had been riding Terry like a rented mule when his heart sputtered and quit bopped in the door. "She wanted to be my ol' lady," Terry said, "but I wasn't having any of that."

A brother jacked her up in the restaurant, dragged her outside and said, "Get out of here. You tried to fuck my brother to death."

Terry experienced his first heart attack at the age of 47 while he was having his way with a beautiful blonde in her second-story Hacienda Heights apartment. "She kicked my ass," Terry said. "I rolled over and couldn't breathe."

In spite of the heart attack Terry continued to smoke. In 2005 he wasn't feeling on top of his game so he strolled into the Arcadia general hospital for a check-up. Upon closer investigation, the doctor's discovered severe blood-flow blockage and induced a coma. Terry wouldn't pull out of it for thirty days. He had endured another mild heart attack, and he also faced artery disease.

He returned home to Hesperia after being released from the hospital, but collapsed the next day. It was a 100-mile journey from Hesperia to Arcadia, "But they had to take me back to the place that broke me," Terry said, so he suffered through the long, winding journey down the 15 freeway through the Cajon pass and into the city.

The doctors discovered a bad arterial junction and they immediately installed a stent. He remained in the hospital another fifteen days, but Vago squads secured his hospital room and monitored his progress.

In his current situation he had no brothers watching his back, so he made a point of not letting many people know his health was failing.

"No sign of weakness ever helps," Terry said. That knowledge didn't stop Terry from smoking though, and his health continued to falter. One heart valve gave out just as he entered prison.

Terry the Tramp did his time and returned to the club a vindicated, loyal brother, albeit broke. He's been approached to join other clubs, but he'll always remain a Vago. Politics will change, brothers will come and go, leaders will stumble, but Terry will always wear green with pride. ☠

"No sign of weakness ever helps," Terry said.

INDEX